D0285432

BODY & SOUL

Body & Soul

*Evangelism
and the Social Concern
of A.B. Simpson*

Daniel J. Evearitt

Daniel J. Evearitt

CHRISTIAN PUBLICATIONS
CAMP HILL, PENNSYLVANIA

Christian Publications
3825 Hartzdale Drive, Camp Hill, PA 17011

The mark of ✝ vibrant faith

ISBN: 0-87509-535-6
LOC Catalog Card Number: 93-72721
© 1994 by Christian Publications
All rights reserved
Printed in the United States of America

94 95 96 97 98 5 4 3 2 1

Cover Design: Step One Design

Unless otherwise indicated, Scripture taken from the
HOLY BIBLE: NEW INTERNATIONAL VERSION®.
© 1973, 1978, 1984 by the International Bible Society.
Used by permission of Zondervan Publishing House.
All rights reserved.

Dedication:

To Karen,

the dearest wife and best friend
anyone could pray for.

CONTENTS

Preface

The seed-thoughts of this book go back to my undergraduate days at Nyack College in the early 1970s. While sitting in a class in Christian doctrines with Paul Collord, I was struck by his reference to the reaction of evangelicals to the "Social Gospel movement" at the turn of the century. He seemed to me to be making excuses for the subsequent years of social neglect by evangelicals that the fundamentalist-modernist controversy of the 1920s initiated. I remember challenging him as to how he could defend what seemed to me—a socially conscious, young, evangelical product of the 1960s—to be the blatant disregard by past generations of the social implications of the gospel of Jesus Christ. He cautioned me to be kind to those of the past, after all we were not in their shoes, nor should we be as critical and judgmental as I was being.

Having been raised in The Christian and Missionary Alliance, I was well aware of the tremendous emphasis the denomination has always placed on world evangelization. What I was not aware of was the significant amount of social work conducted in the early days of the Alliance by A.B. Simpson and his followers. My first inkling of this hidden aspect of my church's roots was while taking Alliance Polity with T. Robert Brewer at Nyack in the spring term of 1970. Passing notice was made of Simpson's outreach to the poor, immigrants, fallen women, and of his rescue mission and orphanage work, which piqued my curiosity.

Years later, after graduating from the newly established Alliance School of Theology and Missions (now Alliance Theological Seminary), and having completed my course work for an M.A. in religious and theological studies at Drew University, I was faced with the task of choosing a topic for my master's thesis. Having ruminated about the social implications of the Christian gospel for a number of years and having done some preliminary exploration in Alliance historical material, I proposed to construct my thesis around the social aspects of the ministry and writings of Albert B. Simpson. The core of the work you now hold is the result of my research into this important and somewhat neglected part of the ministry of Simpson and his compatriots.

I am indebted to my thesis advisor Russell E. Richey for shepherding the project along and for offering a critique and analysis of its content. The thesis review committee included Russ Richey, along with Kenneth E. Rowe and Donald G. Jones; their reading and reaction, reflected in the questions they asked at my oral defense, formed the basis for some modifications that I made in revising the text for publication. Their advice and suggestions were accepted with much gratitude. I would be remiss if I did not acknowledge the encouragement I received from my instructors at Drew University, as well as the late Bard Thompson, who was dean of the graduate school.

The libraries and librarians of Drew University, Nyack College, Alliance Theological Seminary and Columbia University were helpful in providing background material for this work. A special word of thanks is given to John and Woneta Sawin for their help in gathering material on Simpson, when John was archivist and librarian at the A.B. Simpson Historical Library at Christian and Missionary Alliance headquarters in Upper Nyack, N.Y.

I have enjoyed and appreciated the support and encouragement that I have received from the administration, faculty, staff and students at Toccoa Falls College. Special thanks is extended to Gerald E. McGraw and the faculty of the School of Bible and Theology at Toccoa Falls. Their steadfast faithfulness to the Word of God and the cause of Christ has been an inspiration. Doug Matthews was kind enough to let me borrow some of his categories of premillennialism from his doctoral dissertation, for which I am indebted. They helped to bring into sharper focus just where Simpson stood on this issue. Joe M. Sprinkle has been especially helpful as a soundingboard for various ideas and projects, this one included. His patience and advice is greatly appreciated.

K. Neill Foster and Jon Graf at Christian Publications are owed a debt by me for believing in the viability of this project and for their guidance along the way.

Nothing I do in life could ever come about without the care and guidance offered by my wife, Karen. Her love, concern and support helped to sustain me through college, seminary and graduate school, and continues to undergird me as together we seek to serve our Lord.

While various people have had a part in the production of this volume, I alone bear full responsibility for its content, style and any shortcomings.

CHAPTER 1

Introduction

There is room not only for the worship of God, the teaching of sacred truth and the evangelization of the lost, but also for every phase of practical philanthropy and usefulness. There may be, in perfect keeping with the simple order and dignity of the church of God, the most aggressive work for the masses and the widest welcome for every class of sinful men; the ministry of healing for the sick and suffering administered in the name of Jesus; the most complete provision for charitable relief; industrial training and social elevation for the degraded classes, workshops for the unemployed, homes for the orphaned, shelter for the homeless, refuges for the inebriates, the fallen and the helpless; missions for the heathen; Christian literature for the instruction of the people and every agency needed to make the church of God the light of the world and the mothering of the suffering and the lost. And there is no work that will be more glorifying to God than a church that will embrace just such features and completeness.[1]

A.B. Simpson, March, 1893

The common perception of evangelical Christianity in the twentieth century is that it has lacked social concern. Certainly the overwhelming evidence is that evangelicals have largely, by design, neglected social problems throughout much of this century. Such was not always the case. Prior to the 1910s significant social welfare work was conducted by evangelical Christians among the poor, in the cities of America and on the mission field. And a reassessment and reorientation toward social issues has been underway in evangelical circles since the 1960s. A by-product of this reassessment has been a rediscovery of the social attitudes and social outreach programs of evangelicals prior to the fundamentalist-modernist controversy of the 1920s and '30s.

This book deals with A.B. Simpson and the early period of The Christian and Missionary Alliance. It will analyze the effort made by this evangelical leader, and his followers, to relieve social suffering by aiding the victims of the rapid social dislocation that overtook America and the world at the close of the nineteenth century. Simpson and the early Alliance, Timothy Weber has noted, "maintained an unusual balance between old-fashioned evangelism and active social concern."[2] We will examine this balance; what was done in the way of social relief work, why it was done and against what larger theological backdrop it was carried on.

The Background

There was significant social concern among evangelicals in America prior to the Civil War. This has been well documented by Timothy L. Smith in *Revivalism and Social Reform*: "Whatever may have been the role of other factors, the quest for perfection joined with compassion for poor and needy sinners and a rebirth of millennial expectation to make popular Protestantism a mighty social force long before the slavery conflict erupted into war."[3] Smith traced a growth in social concern after the Civil War which led to the Social Gospel movement: "The rapid growth of concern with purely social issues such as poverty, workingman's rights, the liquor traffic, slum housing, and racial bitterness is the chief feature distinguishing American religion after 1865 from that of the first half of the nineteenth century. Such matters in some cases supplanted entirely the earlier pre-occupation with salvation from personal sin and the life hereafter."[4]

Theologically conservative evangelicals objected to the overemphasis by liberal Protestants on the social aspects of the gospel. Because of this they have generally been looked upon by historians as being totally unconcerned with the social issues of their day, concerned only with the salvation of souls. Donald Dayton gives the reason for this prevailing view of conservative evangelicalism in the late nineteenth century. Citing the unavailability of written material on evangelical social work, and the evangelistic tone of the material that does exist, Dayton writes,

> Even if these materials had been widely available, the spirit of the age has not been conducive to an appreciation of revivalistic sects. The triumph of liberal religion after decades of heated controversy, for one thing, did not make for a balanced evaluation of persons of a contrasting persuasion. The bitterness of that controversy, together with the conscious withdrawal of twentieth-century religious conservatives from an emphasis on social welfare, have greatly obscured the larger evangelical contribution to human welfare.[5]

As a consequence, Dayton notes,

> The heroes in the generally accepted picture of the Social Gospel Era have been the small group of Chris-

tian Socialists on the left and the more moderate but much larger number of social gospelers. The villains, in contrast, have been the main body of conservative churchmen on the right, at best irrelevant for the cause of social Christianity and at the worst reactionary. It is with the latter that gospel welfare evangelicals have generally been placed.[6]

Norris Magnuson, in *Salvation in the Slums*, chronicles the efforts of gospel welfare workers in the slums of America at the end of the nineteenth century. The amount of social work done by certain evangelical groups, including The Christian and Missionary Alliance, caused Magnuson to conclude that, "Far from being a hindrance to social Christianity, then, the revivalistic and holiness faith of these people produced extensive social programs and close identification with the needy."[7] John D. Woodbridge, Mark A. Noll and Nathan O. Hatch, in *The Gospel in America*, argue that

> The early twentieth century witnessed considerable evangelical social concern. A goodly number of theological conservatives—increasingly identifying themselves as fundamentalists—actually promoted social witness among the urban poor. A.J. Gordon, founder of the Boston Missionary Training Institute, now Gordon College, and A.C. Dixon, editor of *The Fundamentals*, both were quite active with urban relief programs. A.B. Simpson founded the Christian and Missionary Alliance at the turn of the century not only to promote missions but to serve the largely forgotten poor of the city.[8]

Two Main Categories

Christian social concern has been divided into two main categories, social welfare and social action. "*Social welfare* consists of ministries to help the victims of personal and social problems. It aims at removing or alleviating their suffering by direct treatment of themselves and their environmental circumstances. . . . *Social action* has the goal of changing or reforming basic conditions in society which cause human need. It aims at eliminating the sources of human suffering or, if this is impossible, alleviating the specific conditions which cause it."[9]

A.B. Simpson argued against social action that was directed toward reforming human society. As we shall see, he thought the reformation of society was beyond the role and mission of the church. Just because he did not work toward social reform, however, does not mean that social welfare and relief was not a significant part of his ministry. Although social welfare never took the place of evangelism, Simpson consistently urged Christians not to ignore the human suffering they encountered, but to do something about it.

The Major Shift

What happened to this evangelical social concern and identification with needy peoples? Why were Christian relief efforts curtailed? David Moberg, in *The Great Reversal: Evangelism versus Social Concern*, writes, "From approximately 1910 until the 1930s, however, a major shift in the position of evangelicals on social issues occurred, a shift which historian Timothy L. Smith has termed 'the Great Reversal' in some of his lectures."[10]

Evangelicals, seeking to avoid the taint of the liberal social gospel of their day, withdrew from active social welfare activity.

Moberg saw the cause for the decline of social concern among evangelical groups coming about, in part, because of "the premillennialist doctrine that all social conditions would inevitably and irresistibly grow increasingly worse until the Second Coming of Jesus Christ, the belief that only the establishment of the millennial Kingdom of Christ could cure social problems."[11]

Carl F.H. Henry, in his seminal book *The Uneasy Conscience of Modern Fundamentalism* in 1947, noted that, premillennialists "are convinced not only that non-evangelicals cannot bring in the perfect social order . . . . but also that the evangelicals will not bring it in by their proclamation of the Gospel. This latter conviction is grounded in the belief that the inauguration of the kingdom awaits the second advent of Christ in His visible return."[12] While some evangelicals at the turn of the century were attracted to the social gospel movement, Henry claims, "the great majority cut loose deliberately from the social reform movements of the times, denounced as futile and deceptive the world-changing efforts on a non-Biblical formula, and redoubled their efforts to rescue the minority from an increasingly hostile environment."[13] The abandonment of social welfare work by evangelicals was not, according to Henry, a logical necessity. To be true to its own principles, Henry argued, evangelicalism must consistently assert "1) That Christianity opposes any and every evil, personal and social, and must never be represented as in any way tolerant of such evil; 2) That Christianity opposes such evil, as the only sufficient formula for its resolution, the redemptive work of Jesus Christ and the regenerative work of the Holy Spirit." Henry strongly rejects the charge that the Fundamentalist ideology logically involves an indifference to social evils, and presses the contention that the non-evangelical ideology involves an essential inability to right the world order.[14]

Do all premillennialists see social welfare work as something evangelicals should avoid? Not necessarily, says Douglas K. Matthews, in his insightful doctoral dissertation "Approximating the Millennium: Toward a Coherent Premillennial Theology of Social Transformation." He presents four major categories of premillennial social theory and places A.B. Simpson on the spectrum. It will be helpful to look at Matthews' four categories in order to understand Simpson's social theory in juxtaposition to other premillennialist evangelicals.

Antagonistic Premillennialism, Matthews states, asserts that "any attempts to improve the world were Satanic and would pave the way for the Antichrist. Any form of social concern often was equated with a 'false' social gospel." Some premillennialists at the turn of the century believed "that social reform, such as the temperance movement, would actually hinder or slow down Christ's return. In this view social degeneration would actually provoke or serve as sure evidence of the Parousia."[15] Why try to improve social conditions? This might only serve to postpone Christ's return. Matthews notes that an "extremely pessimistic or fatalistic premillennial theology would tend to undergird" those holding this antagonistic premillennialist viewpoint.[16]

Anticorrosive or Preservative Premillennialism has been more prevalent since World War II. "This alternative is generally suspicious of massive social improvements, but is very convinced of the need to halt the corruption of the church and society, especially in America," Matthews points out. Since human history is in its last phase, real progress is unattainable. The best that can be hoped for is that, "Social conditions can only be improved in the sense of not getting worse."[17]

Transformational Premillennialists, Matthews concludes, "are convinced that world conditions can be improved, although not on a utopian scale, prior to the Second Coming."[18] "Simply put, the transformational premillennialist believes that the structures, character, and conditions of society at large can be significantly improved. . . . the key point here is that large-scale positive change initiated by the church is possible."[19] His dissertation goes on to present the case for the validity and viability of transformational premillennialism.

Matthews places A.B. Simpson in the category of social theory he labels *Relief-Oriented Premillennialism*. The focus of this type of premillennialism is on helping the suffering victims of social ills; Matthews also labels this *Symptomatic Premillennialism*, because the symptoms and results of social ills are dealt with, but not the root causes. He asserts, "Premillennial efforts in this area have been commendable, significant, courageous, widespread, and have included the following: faith missions, work among the poor and unchurched, rescue missions, work with prisoners, work in hospitals, and literacy campaigns."[20] He gives as his prime example of relief-oriented premillennialism, "A.B. Simpson, who shifted from postmillennialism to premillennialism early in his ministry, excelled in this type of relief work, yet after embracing premillennialism he seemed to view social degeneration as inevitable and was more than skeptical of attempts to alter social structures."[21] Simpson engaged in social relief work without any expectation that society could be transformed. Just because significant social modification was out of the question for Simpson, does not mean that he did not see the alleviation of the effects of social corruption and disfunction as a part of the ministry of the church.

In an attempt to uncover the forgotten history of Simpson and other late-nineteenth century evangelicals, George Marsden, in his landmark book *Fundamentalism and American Culture*, wrote to "correct the impression that revivalist evangelicals of this era were overwhelmingly complacent and inactive on social questions." He pointed out that D.L. Moody and other premillennial and holiness evangelists "led in preserving the tradition of evangelical social work. Though they were dedicated first to saving souls, greatly occupied with personal piety, and held pessimistic social views, their record of Christian social service, in an era when social reform was not popular, was as impressive as that of almost any group in the country."[22]

The Liberal Over-emphasis

Premillennialism, then, partly explains the reversal from active social relief to social inaction by many evangelicals in the early twentieth century. But another contributing factor was the rejection by conservative evangelicals of the predominant liberal-modernist over-emphasis upon a social salvation that precluded personal salvation. This was coupled with a reaction by evangelicals against liberal theological criticism of such cherished doctrines as the inerrancy and inspiration of the Bible, the miracles of Jesus and other fundamental Christian doctrines strongly held by conservatives.

Evangelical Christians were labeled "fundamentalists" after *The Fundamentals,* a series of books defending basic Christian doctrines, was published between 1910 and 1915. Fundamentalism is a term "employed disparagingly by its foes and proudly by its adherents. It designates those who, in reaction to modernist theology, hold tenaciously to the fundamentals of orthodox Christianity. The movement is as much a mood and reaction as it is a theological system, and it is indeed its reactionary spirit that has given it bad press."[23]

That evangelicals over-reacted to the liberal social gospel, by almost totally withdrawing from any significant social welfare work, is obvious to us at the end of the twentieth century. However, those at the helm of evangelical organizations in that day were dealing with some very real fears and challenges. Before their eyes many formerly solid evangelical denominations, mission boards, colleges and seminaries were rejecting traditional beliefs, questioning the authority of the Bible and embracing the social gospel. As a result, anything that hinted at social involvement was shunned by evangelicals. Premillennial social theory, as well as the strong reaction against liberal-modernism's rejection of key doctrinal truths and personal salvation in favor of social reform, galvanized evangelical Christians in the 1920s in their overwhelming rejection of social welfare work.

Simpson's Work Obscured

The "Great Reversal" discussed by Smith and Moberg occurred mostly after the death of A.B. Simpson; therefore, the main thrust of this book will be to uncover the lost history of social involvement by Simpson and his early followers which has been obscured by subsequent events. There was a significant level of social activity around Simpson's ministry that has largely been forgotten. Forgotten as well are the theological underpinnings that caused Simpson and his associates to engage in social work. The purpose of this book will be to find out what happened, to examine why it happened and to judge the value of the theology behind what happened. Hopefully this will enlighten contemporary evangelical Christians about the social concern and social relief that is a part of their history and highlight the continued need for social concern among evangelicals today.

Two earlier works have discussed the social relief work of Simpson and his associates, John V. Dahms' chapter "The Social Interest and Concern of A.B. Simpson," in *The Birth of a Vision*,[24] and the centennial history of The Christian and Missionary Alliance, *All For Jesus*, written by Robert L. Niklaus, John S. Sawin and Samuel J. Stoesz.[25] The bulk of the material contained in the present work was gathered before the appearance of the above works. It grew out of a masters thesis completed at The Graduate School of Drew University in 1980. The genesis of this work dates back to my days as a student at Nyack College where I first heard vague references to social relief work conducted by A.B. Simpson during the early days of The Christian and Missionary Alliance. My effort to seek out this lost heritage has resulted in the work which you now hold in your hands.

Endnotes

1. A.B. Simpson, "The Ministering Church," *The Christian Alliance and Missionary Weekly* 13 Mar. 1893: 165.

2. Timothy P. Weber, *Living in the Shadow of the Second Coming: American Premillennialism 1875-1925* (New York: Oxford Univ. Press, 1979) 78.

3. Timothy L. Smith, *Revivalism and Social Reform* (New York: Abingdon Press, 1957) 149.

4. Smith 148.

5. Donald Dayton, foreword, *Salvation in the Slums* by Norris Magnuson (Metuchen, N.J.: Scarecrow Press, 1977) x-xi.

6. Dayton xii.

7. Norris Magnuson, *Salvation in the Slums* (Metuchen, N.J.: Scarecrow Press, 1977) 178.

8. John D. Woodbridge, Mark A. Noll and Nathan O. Hatch, *The Gospel in America: Themes in the Story of America's Evangelicals* (Grand Rapids: Zondervan, 1979) 240.

9. David Moberg, *Inasmuch: Christian Social Responsibility in the Twentieth Century* (Grand Rapids: Eerdmans, 1965) 81.

10. David Moberg, *The Great Reversal: Evangelism versus Social Concern* (New York: J.B. Lippincott, 1972) 31.

11. Moberg 37.
12. Carl F.H. Henry, *The Uneasy Conscience of Modern Fundamentalism* (Grand Rapids: Eerdmans, 1947) 28-29.
13. Henry 33.
14. Henry 45.
15. Douglas K. Matthews, "Approximating the Millennium: Toward a Coherent Premillennial Theology of Social Transformation," diss., Baylor University, 1992: 61-62.
16. Matthews 63.
17. Matthews 65.
18. Matthews 70.
19. Matthews 71.
20. Matthews 63.
21. Matthews 63.
22. George M. Marsden, *Fundamentalism and American Culture: The Shaping of Twentieth-Century Evangelicalism: 1870-1925* (New York: Oxford Univ. Press, 1980) 85.
23. Dennis P. Hollinger, *Individualism and Social Ethics: An Evangelical Syncretism* (Lanham, MD: University Press of America, 1983) 58.
24. John V. Dahms, "The Social Interest and Concern of A.B. Simpson," *The Birth of a Vision*, ed. David F. Hartzfeld and Charles Nienkirchen (Beaverlodge, Alberta: Buena Book Services, 1986) 49-74.
25. Robert K. Niklaus, John S. Sawin and Samuel J. Stoesz, *All For Jesus: God at Work in the Christian and Missionary Alliance Over One Hundred Years* (Camp Hill, PA: Christian Publications, 1986).

CHAPTER 2

The Life of A.B. Simpson

I have now, O Lord, as Thou hast said in Thy Word, covenanted with Thee, not for worldly honors or fame but for everlasting life, and I know that Thou art true and shall never break Thy holy Word. Give to me now all the blessings of the New Covenant and especially the Holy Spirit in great abundance, which is the earnest of my inheritance until the redemption of the purchased possession. May a double portion of Thy Spirit rest upon me, and then I shall go and proclaim to transgressors Thy ways and Thy laws to the people. Sanctify me wholly and make me fit for heaven. Give me all spiritual blessing, in heavenly places in Christ Jesus.

Place me in what circumstances Thou mayest desire; but if it be Thy holy will, I desire that Thou "give me neither poverty nor riches; feed me with food convenient, lest I be poor and steal, or lest I be rich and say, Who is the Lord? But thy will be done. Now give me Thy Spirit and Thy protection in my heart at all times, and then I shall drink of the rivers of salvation, lie down by still waters, and be infinitely happy in the favor of my God." (January 19, 1861)

Those who are already familiar with the life and ministry of A.B. Simpson and the founding years of The Christian and Missionary Alliance may choose to skim through this chapter.

Those unfamiliar with Simpson's life and ministry will find a brief overview of the life of one of the world's foremost evangelical leaders of the late-nineteenth and early-twentieth centuries.

Albert Benjamin Simpson was born on December 15, 1843 in Bayview, Prince Edward Island, Canada.[1] When he was three years old his family moved to Kent County in Western Ontario where Albert grew up and attended school.[2] His parents, James and Jane Simpson, were Scotch-Presbyterian. His father was an elder in the Presbyterian church; his mother was an avid reader of classical poetry.[3]

The household was deeply religious. A.W. Tozer, one of Simpson's biographers, notes, "The parents had set themselves to bring up their children after the manner of their Scottish forbears. Sharp discipline, stern rules, severe restraint upon conduct, all these young Albert knew, with big chunks of theology which he confessed later he could not understand, crammed into his head daily. Then there was church, family prayer, the catechism, and long dry books by reforming fathers, more prayer and church again."[4]

It was in this religious atmosphere that Albert began to think about becoming a minister. He secretly held this desire to himself from the age of ten.[5] At the age of fourteen Albert learned that the ministry was not in the plans his father had laid out for the family. Howard, the eldest son, was to enter the ministry while Albert was to stay at home to help on the farm. This news was a crushing blow to hopes young Albert had to become a minister. He begged and pleaded that his father reconsider and allow him to prepare for the ministry. Even though he was physically frail he vowed to raise money to pay for his own education. His father finally agreed that if Albert felt so strongly about his call to preach he could follow that course.[6]

Entering the Ministry

Simpson appeared before the presbytery of London, Ontario on October 1, 1861 along with other young men and was approved to commence study for the ministry.[7] He entered Knox College in Toronto that same month where he studied for four years, during which time he supplied student pulpits in the summers.[8] He graduated from Knox College in April, 1865 and was examined by the presbytery of Toronto for licensing in the areas of "Hebrew, Greek, Theology, Church History and Church Government, as well as personal religion."[9]

Simpson received a call from Knox Church, Hamilton, Ontario on August 15, 1865 which he accepted. He was ordained there on Sunday, September the 11th, and on Tuesday of that week he was married to Margaret Henry.[10] All this at the age of twenty-one.

The ministry at Knox Church was a fruitful one where, over the course of his eight years there, Simpson saw 750 members added to the church fellowship. Calls were extended to him from Knox Church, Ottawa; Chalmers Church, Quebec; and Chestnut Street, Louisville in December of 1873. He chose Louisville over the others, partially because of the fairer climate, leaving Knox Church, Hamilton on December 20, 1873.[11]

The Louisville Years

Chestnut Street Church in Louisville, Kentucky in January 1874 was the largest Presbyterian church in town. Simpson began his ministry there, as he described it, "still treading the well beaten paths of the modern church."[12]

The city still suffered from the effects of the recently concluded Civil War, with bitterness and hatred still a strong disruptive factor. Feeling that this was hindering spiritual growth, Simpson invited all of the city's ministers to Chestnut Street Church where he proposed that an outside evangelist be brought in to hold union meetings. This approach was agreed upon resulting in evangelistic services conducted by the well-known evangelist Major Whittle and the gospel singer P.P. Bliss. The meetings evolved into regular Sunday evening evangelistic services held in large halls, and eventually, to a tabernacle being built to house the large crowds drawn in each week.[13]

Simpson was deeply touched by the message of Major Whittle which "awakened him to his lack of spiritual power for life and service and led him to seek the infilling of the Holy Spirit."[14]

He also became interested in world evangelization during this period of his life. This interest was heightened by a disturbing dream he had of millions of lost souls who "in mute anguish were wringing their hands, and their faces wore an expression I can never forget."[15] Due to his intense concern for world missions Simpson envisioned an illustrated missionary magazine to inform people about world evangelism and to arouse young people to the call of foreign missions. He believed New York City to be the best possible place from which to publish such a journal. With this in mind, he eagerly accepted a call which came from the Thirteenth Street Church, New York City, beginning his ministry there in November of 1879.[16]

The Social Concern Grows

Simpson's ministry in New York began with an optimistic increase in church attendance as well as many converts being added to the fellowship. However, problems started to develop when the pastor began to "show so much interest in the poor and lost of the city streets."[17] The members of the church were interested in building up their church but they felt that the church should not be a rescue mission. The members were "well-to-do people, fairly along toward the top of the social ladder." They welcomed any member who was of their own kind.[18]

The pastor's ideas about what the church should be clashed significantly with what the members thought their church should be. "His vision was bigger than one church, his love deeper than one social stratum. He wanted his church to give up its narrow exclusiveness and become a center for the evangelization of the masses."[19]

When Simpson proposed to the session that over one hundred of his converts from the poor Italian quarters be allowed to worship at Thirteenth Street, things began to come to a head. The session kindly suggested that the Italians might be happier in a church of their own class and rejected his plan to bring them into their prosperous, higher class church.[20]

Later in life, reflecting on his ministry at Thirteenth Street Church, Simpson recalled the two years as cordial and congenial ones, yet ones that found him at odds with the church members who "could not adjust themselves to the radical and aggressive measures to which God was leading me. What they wanted was a conventional parish for respectable Christians. What their young pastor wanted was a multitude of publicans and sinners."[21]

This factor, plus disagreements over believer versus infant baptism and church amusements, led Simpson to sever ties with Thirteenth Street Church Presbyterian Church.[22]

"His decision to quit his church and strike out alone into the work of evangelizing the multitudes of New York looked to everyone except A.B. Simpson like a piece of rare folly. He had been earning five thousand dollars a year at his old job. Now he had exactly no income at all, and a family of seven to support."[23]

Independent Work

Resigning his church in November of 1881 he immediately began to hold evangelistic services in Caledonia Hall, a dance hall on Thirteenth Street, which led on February 10, 1882 to the organizing of an independent church.[24] After moving to numerous locations in New York the Gospel Tabernacle, as the church was called, moved into newly constructed facilities on Eighth Avenue at the corner of 44th Street in 1889.[25]

The constitution and bylaws of the organization laid out in February of 1882 follow:

1. The Word of God alone shall be the rule of doctrine, practice and discipline in this church; it being always understood that we receive it as the inspired Word of God, and the only divine rule of faith and conduct.

2. That we recognize and receive the Lord Jesus Christ as the true and divine Son of the living God, the only Head of the Church and our only Saviour, and Master; and the Holy Spirit in His divine personality as the only source and channel of all true spiritual life and power.

3. That we recognize in Christian fellowship and affection the one Church of God, consisting of all true believers of whatever name, and that we desire to stand in Christian communion with every organization of evangelical Christians who hold and practice the truth as it is in Jesus, and are organized and constituted in accordance with the Word of God, for the work of the Gospel.

4. While we recognize it as our high calling, in connection with every true church of Christ, to worship and witness for God and His truth, and to cherish, nurture and edify His children, and to build up His kingdom; yet it will ever be recognized as the specific mission of this church to promote the work of evangelization among the neglected classes at home and abroad, as God may enable us in every part of the world.

5. The profession of living faith in the Lord Jesus Christ, a sincere purpose to live according to His will and for His glory; and the evidence of consistent moral and Christian character and life, will be the only condition of membership in this church.

6. New members will be received at the regular monthly business meeting on the recommendation of the Pastor and Elders, on their public confession of faith and vote of the members.

7. The ordinance of baptism will be administered on profession of faith and ordinarily by immersion. Persons who have been baptized otherwise, or in infancy, will be received if they are satisfied with their own baptism. Parents will have the privilege of presenting their infant children in the house of God for public consecration to God.

8. The Lord's Supper will be administered not less frequently than once every month on the second Lord's day of the month.[26]

As can be seen by the above, one of the basic thrusts of Simpson's independent work was the evangelization of "neglected classes" both in the United States and abroad. He did not seek another new denomination to work in the tried and tested areas of church work, but rather sought out people who were being overlooked by traditional church programs.

Two separate organizations grew from Simpson's vision of world evangelization. The Christian Alliance was founded to work in North America to enrich the Church by emphasizing what Simpson called "The Fourfold Gospel"—Christ as Savior, Sanctifier, Healer and Coming King. The Evangelical Missionary Alliance was founded as a world missions organization to train, send out and support foreign missionaries. Both of these organizations came into existence at a convention held in Old Orchard, Maine in 1887. They merged in 1897 to form The Christian and Missionary Alliance.[27]

The Missionary Training Institute had already begun the task of training missionaries and Christian workers. Established by Simpson in 1882, the Institute was the first such Bible school in North America which remains in existence today. At the turn of the century it was moved from New York City to Nyack, New York.[28]

Simpson's Theology

The basic theology of A.B. Simpson and The Christian and Missionary Alliance can be found in his book *The Fourfold Gospel.* Jesus Christ is seen as Savior. He ransomed mankind from the power and guilt of sin through His substitutionary atonement on Calvary's cross, giving believers a new heart and favor with God, not based on what man does, rather, on what Christ did in His death and resurrection. Individuals procure this salvation by being convicted of sin, seeing Christ as their only hope of salvation, repenting and turning from sin, accepting Christ as their Savior and living and abiding in Christ.[29] In declaring Christ as Sanctifier, Simpson saw full salvation as not merely regeneration but total separation from sin, this evil world and one's own sinful self, dedicating one's life and will to God and loving God above all else. This was purchased by Christ and given to believers as a free gift as the Holy Spirit came to dwell in one's life.[30] Christ as Healer signifies the healing power of God brought to believers as a result of Christ's death. It is the "supernatural Divine power of God infused into human bodies, renewing the weakness of suffering human frames by the life and power of God."[31] Christ our Coming King means a physical return of the victorious Jesus Christ to earth in a visible manner to set up his millennial kingdom.[32] Simpson was a strong believer in the return of Christ to earth to set up His millennial kingdom.

The four basic doctrines of Simpson's theology did not come to him overnight. The individual items are not unique to him or to The Christian and Missionary Alliance. Yet in combination they form a distinctive theology shared by Simpson, his organization and like-minded Christians before the turn of the century. A conservative tradition of belief in the personal salvation of the individual from sin to full dedication to God, through the sanctifying power of the Holy Spirit, availing oneself of the healing power of Christ and looking forward to His return to earth in like manner as He had departed, formed the core of Simpson's message. Simpson tied his theology to a strong emphasis on sharing Christ and His gospel with a lost and dying world.

The elements of his theology parallel somewhat his own spiritual development. As a young man Simpson had struggled with personal salvation; at Louisville he had struggled with sanctification and the infilling of the Holy Spirit; ill health had plagued him throughout his life, leading him to the doctrine of divine healing in Scripture; and signs of the times, coupled with studies of scriptural prophecies, led him to believe that he was living in the last days and that at any moment Christ might reappear.[33]

Simpson shared much of his theology, his pulpit and the pages of his periodicals with such like-minded preachers as "F.B. Meyer, A.J. Gordon, A.T. Pierson, D.L. Moody, Charles A. Blanchard, R.A. Torrey, James M. Gray, Robert E. Speer, J. Wilbur Chapman, Charles Trumbull, and a host of others."[34]

He led The Christian and Missionary Alliance, traveled on missionary tours, edited magazines, wrote hundreds of articles and over eighty books, lectured at the Missionary Training Institute, wrote many hymns, held evangelistic meetings nationwide and served on the board of trustees of several rescue missions for over thirty years.[35]

Simpson's rigorous schedule continued until 1917 when his pace slowed somewhat. He suffered a stroke in the spring of 1919 and spent the summer in and around his home in Nyack. On October 28, 1919, after a session of prayer for missionaries, he fell into a coma. He died on the morning of October 29, 1919.[36]

Endnotes

1. A.E. Thompson, *A.B. Simpson: His Life and Work* (Harrisburg: Christian Publications, 1920 revised 1960) 3.
2. G.P. Pardington, *Twenty-five Wonderful Years 1889-1914* (New York: Christian Alliance Publishing Co., 1914) 18.
3. Samuel J. Stoesz, *Understanding My Church* (Harrisburg: Christian Publications, 1968) 76.

4. A.W. Tozer, *Wingspread: A.B. Simpson: A Study in Spiritual Altitude* (Harrisburg: Christian Publications, 1943) 17.
5. Stoesz 76.
6. Tozer 20.
7. Thompson 31.
8. Thompson 41-42.
9. Thompson 42.
10. Thompson 42.
11. Thompson 50-51.
12. Thompson 53.
13. Thompson 54-55.
14. Thompson 65; considerable disagreement exists over the issue of when Simpson's deeper life crisis/infilling of the Holy Spirit took place. Two interesting works which examine this question are Samuel J. Stoesz's *Sanctification: An Alliance Distinctive* (Camp Hill, PA: Christian Publications, 1992), and Gerald E. McGraw's unpublished doctoral dissertation, "The Doctrine of Sanctification in the Published Writings of Albert Benjamin Simpson," New York University, 1986, (available from University Microfilms International, Ann Arbor, MI).
15. Tozer 62.
16. Tozer 67.
17. Tozer 67.
18. Tozer 68.
19. Tozer 68.
20. Tozer 69.
21. Thompson 85.
22. Thompson 85-86.
23. Tozer 86.
24. Pardington 25-26.
25. Pardington 28.

26. Stoesz 79-80.
27. Stoesz 83-85.
28. Stoesz 175.
29. A.B. Simpson, *The Fourfold Gospel* (Harrisburg: Christian Publications, 1925) 12-20.
30. Simpson *Fourfold* 33-40.
31. Simpson *Fourfold* 56.
32. Simpson *Fourfold* 73-78.
33. Thompson 75-76.
34. Stoesz 81.
35. Tozer 131.
36. Tozer 140-142.

CHAPTER 3

The Religious Climate in Which A.B. Simpson Lived

Philanthropic schemes and social reforms are absorbing the interest and enthusiasm of thousands of redeemed men and women who ought to be giving their strength and wealth to the best things and not the second best. We admit there is something good in these enterprises. They have a place and a value, but let the world take care of them. . . . If God has given you a higher calling show it by engaging in higher work. There are plenty of people to build the universities and endow them; plenty of people to run social reform and temperance societies; plenty of people to fight the political battle. God wants you to give the Gospel to the world, to rise to the highest calling, to do the best things. (October 27, 1897)

The theological basis of A.B. Simpson's social ministry cannot be understood without first examining the religious setting in which it was formed. He was carrying over many of the older traditional emphases which were under attack at the close of the nineteenth century. Some of his statements are in direct response to the challenges to what he held to be "true Christianity." Therefore it becomes important to look at a brief survey of some of the ideas popularized in American Protestantism between the Civil War and World War I.

A Change in Emphasis

In *The Social Gospel: Religion and Reform in Changing America*, White and Hopkins speak of a change of emphasis in American Protestantism during this period. "A dominant evangelical tradition long emphasized an individual salvation. Now the church was awakening to the possibilities of social salvation as well."[1] They note that, "The rapid shift of concern with purely social issues such as poverty, workingman's rights, the liquor traffic, slum housing, and racial bitterness is the chief feature distinguishing American religion after 1865 from that of the first half of the nineteenth century."[2]

Robert Handy writes, of the last part of the nineteenth century, "much of the real focus had shifted to civilization itself, with Christianity and the churches finding their significance in relation to it."[3] Handy concludes from his survey of the period that, "Most Protestants in the America of 1890 saw themselves as belonging to the national religion, a religion of civilization."[4]

Both of these assessments can be supported by looking at the religious books being published at the end of the nineteenth century. They show a decided swing toward social salvation and toward perfecting society.

Josiah Strong, a leader of the social gospel movement, an advocate of Americanism and proponent of urban ministries, in *The Next Great Awakening* (1902), argued against the older ideas of personal salvation and the expectation of the kingdom of God being achieved only in heaven. He wrote, "The common belief in the kingdom of God has been like many men's belief in immortality—something ghostly, mysterious, intangible and vague; . . . identical with heaven."[5] He pointed out that with the older religion, "The great object is to 'save the soul.' It results naturally in a subjective type of religion, and an individualistic Christianity."[6] Strong wrote that, "Now the kingdom of God is the synthesis of religion and morals, of Christianity and philanthropy."[7] To which he added, "The kingdom of God is Utopia made rational and destined to be actual. It is the new social ideal perfected. It is the New Jerusalem, come down from God out of heaven and resplendent with His glory."[8]

A Perfected Society

In *The Twentieth Century City*, Strong spoke of a perfected society on earth, a world where the will of God is done, where all is peace and harmony. He wrote of this realizable goal, "The new social ideal, dim and imperfect, when fully focused, is seen to be the kingdom of heaven for which our Lord taught us daily to pray, and which he bade us to seek first."[9] He found this social hope in the "three great laws of the Kingdom of God" as taught by Jesus: service, sacrifice and love. He argued that, "the religion of Jesus is profoundly social, and as perfectly adapted to the saving of society as if that were its only object."[10] Strong's view of the salvation Christ came to procure was much broader than traditional Protestant soteriology. His was, "not a gospel for isolated individuals, but one for men in an organized society, a kingdom coming in the earth."[11]

Washington Gladden, in *How Much Is Left of the Old Doctrines?*, wrote along similar lines. He believed that men who are shown a higher way to live will be able to live that way. Of conversion he wrote, "They must highly resolve that henceforth the law of the mind, and not the law of the members, shall bear rule in their lives, that by God's grace they will become the men and women that they ought to be." What they needed was determination and a better environment in order to become better people.[12] When this came about on a world-wide scale,

Gladden wrote, "I can imagine no heaven brighter than this world would be if sin and its consequences were abolished."[13]

The president of the New York Association for the Poor, R. Fulton Cutting, in his 1912 book *The Church and Society*, dismissed the older theology: "The Church's theory has been that the way to moralize Society is to increase the number of the elect. Has she not made a mistake in the order of precedence? May she not increase the number of the elect more rapidly by moralizing Society?"[14] Cutting thought that the church of the future should be seeking after the ideal society. He wrote,

> Utopian as it seems, it is quite probable that vice and crime might be practically eliminated from civilization by an intelligent and sympathetic training of the child in morals and obedience to the law; but this would require the ideal Church, the ideal parent, and the ideal school. It is just such ideals that the Church should always keep before her.[15]

George Hodges, in *Faith and Social Service*, wrote, "The problem of the city is a Christian problem, and it needs Christian men to solve it. The purpose of it is to make the city better that its people may be better. It would save men's bodies for the sake of their souls."[16]

Chauncey B. Brewster, a Connecticut clergyman, in his book *The Kingdom of God and American Life*, written in 1912, noted that the idea of the kingdom goes beyond the church: ". . . while its chief organ is the Church, that kingdom touches and lays hold of, and embraces in its scope other institutions, the Family, the State, . . . It means a social order as wide as human existence."[17]

The New Redemption written by George D. Herron in 1893

also takes social salvation beyond the church to the state. Herron believed that, "The social problem is the call of the state to become Christian."[18] He saw the social turmoil in America at the close of the 19th century as an opportunity for the church to reform society. "The social revolution . . . is the call and opportunity of Christendom to become Christian. The whole social problem is a question of how to manifest Christianity as the natural humanity of man; how to reveal the cross as the universal law of sacrifice by which God made and redeemed the world."[19] Herron saw Christ's mission and his salvation as a social theology. Jesus Christ came as the bearer of a new social order based on love and sacrifice, which he proved by his crucifixion.[20] He noted, "The love of Christ was the most revolutionary element that had ever been introduced into society."[21] Arguing against personal salvation as the purpose of Christ's death, he wrote, "Salvation is not a change of worlds, but a change of the moral basis of life; . . . Heaven is a quality of life." Salvation is a change of attitude.[22] He emphatically stated, "There can be no peace on earth until the kingdoms of this world are become the kingdoms of God's Christ, and the cross of Christ has become the law of the world's life."[23] Herron also saw the church as the chief agent of social redemption, but, "If the church that accepts Christ's name refuses to bear his cross of social redemption, it will justify the statement that it is not a Christian institution, and God will regenerate civilization without the church."[24]

Walter Rauschenbusch, probably the most widely read of the social gospel theologians, also shared this concern about social rather than personal salvation. In *Christianizing the Social Order*, he wrote, "The Christian Church in the past has taught us to do our work with our eyes fixed on another world and a life to come. But the business before us is concerned with refashioning this present world, making this earth clean and sweet and habitable."[25] Personal salvation was to be found in social service.[26] He believed that Christ's mission was to redeem society. "Jesus worked on individuals and through individuals, but his real end was not individualistic but social."[27] He argued, "It is not a matter of getting individuals to heaven, but of transforming the life on earth into the harmony of heaven."[28] The kingdom of God is here and now, not off in some distant future.[29] Rauschenbusch issued a challenge, "Do we dare to undertake the readjustment of all social life to bring it into obedience to the law of love?"[30] He saw this as a greater challenge than believing in old, irrelevant dogmas.

So, the older theology of personal salvation, with the kingdom of God off in the future, was to be left behind by the new social theology of the late 19th century. As James Dombrowski has noted, "The most prominent feature of the Social Gospel is its emphasis upon the saving of society rather than upon the salvation of individuals."[31]

Charles Hopkins has asserted that, "America's most unique contribution to the great ongoing stream of Christianity is the social gospel."[32] In *The Rise of the Social Gospel in American Protestantism 1865-1915*, Hopkins traced the social gospel back to the Puritan settler's efforts to create a new heaven and earth in America. This notion was then picked up by Horace Bushnell, Henry Ward Beecher and Phillips Brooks and, eventually, was given voice by Washington Gladden, Josiah Strong and Walter Rauschenbusch.

The Overlooked Role of Revivalism

To this overall picture of Protestantism in the late 19th century Timothy L. Smith added the overlooked role of revivalism in producing the social gospel. Revivalism brought to Protestantism, according to Smith, some essential elements. "Lay leadership, the drive toward interdenominational fellowship, the primacy of ethics over dogma, and the democratization of Calvinism were more nearly the fruits of fervor than of reflection."[33] Smith noted the changes that came rapidly upon American religion after the Civil War, especially the increased emphasis upon social salvation, with a shift away from personal salvation.[34] He asserted that revivalism heightened belief in the perfectibility of man and compassion for the poor and needy.[35] He found that the main thrust of evangelists in post-Civil War America was still personal salvation and preparation for the hereafter.[36] Social issues took second place to personal salvation in revivalism; however, Smith still credited revivalism with a significant role in promoting social change. "If God seemed near in nineteenth-century America, it was not because an elite circle of theologians read Darwin's book on *The Descent of Man*." Rather, Smith claimed, "It was due to the fact that in countless revivals the 'tongues of fire' had descended on the disciples, freeing them from the bondage of sin and selfishness, and dedicating them to the task of making over the world."[37]

A Heaven on Earth

The religious climate in America at the close of the 19th century was one of optimism in the midst of staggering change. The growth of cities, the rapid expansion of industry, the enormous wealth of a handful of individuals, the influx of European immigrants, the challenge of socialism and Darwinism, the rise of higher biblical criticism and doubts about supernaturalism all moved the mainstream of Protestantism toward the social gospel. There was a fervent hope that the church could reform society by calling humanity to live according to the higher principles of love, service and sacrifice. The kingdom of God could be ushered in if the church worked to save society. Society could become a heaven on earth. The shift was away from the older doctrines of personal sin and salvation to an emphasis on social sin and social salvation. This new theology relied on a belief in humanity's ability to better itself, rather than God's redemptive intervention to save individuals.

Where Simpson Stood

Nothing could be more opposed to the gospel message that A.B. Simpson was faithfully preaching during these same years than this liberal, social salvation message. While postmillennial social gospelers were heralding the dawn of a new era of peace, prosperity and a Christianized world, a premillennialist Simpson was forecasting the decline and degeneration of human society prior to the triumphant Second Coming of Jesus Christ. While social gospel advocates were constructing grand schemes to reform society, Simpson was seeking lost souls, offering them the hope of the saving gospel of Jesus Christ and alleviating human suffering and physical need.

Endnotes

1. Ronald C. White and C. Ronald Hopkins, *The Social Gospel: Religion and Reform in Changing America* (Philadelphia: Temple University Press, 1976) 3.
2. White and Hopkins 6.
3. Robert T. Handy, *A Christian America: Protestant Hopes and Historical Realities* (New York: Oxford University Press, 1971) 110.
4. Handy 115.
5. Josiah Strong, *The Next Great Awakening* (New York: The Baker & Taylor Co., 1902) 59.

6. Strong 60.
7. Strong 109.
8. Strong 115.
9. Josiah Strong, *The Twentieth Century City* (New York: The Baker & Taylor Co., 1898) 121-122.
10. Strong *Twentieth* 127-128.
11. Strong *Twentieth* 146.
12. Washington Gladden, *How Much Is Left of the Old Doctrines?* (Boston: Houghton, Mifflin, 1899) 239.
13. Gladden 307.
14. R. Fulton Cutting, *The Church and Society* (New York: Macmillan, 1912) 36.
15. Cutting 35.
16. George Hodges, *Faith and Social Service* (New York: Thomas Whittaker, 1896) 241.
17. Chauncey B. Brewster, *The Kingdom of God and American Life* (New York: Thomas Whittaker, 1912) 32.
18. George D. Herron, *The New Redemption* (New York: Thomas Y. Crowell & Co., 1893) 30.
19. Herron 41.
20. Herron 80-81.
21. Herron 83.
22. Herron 104.
23. Herron 85.
24. Herron 97.
25. Walter Rauschenbusch, *Christianizing the Social Order* (New York: Macmillan, 1912) 42.
26. Walter Rauschenbusch, *Unto Me* (Boston: Pilgrim Press, 1912) 20.
27. Walter Rauschenbusch, *Christianity and the Social Crisis* (New York: Macmillan, 1907) 61.
28. Rauschenbusch *Crisis* 65.

29. Rauschenbusch *Crisis* 65.

30. Walter Rauschenbusch, *Dare We Be Christians?* (Boston: Pilgrim Press, 1914) 24-25.

31. James Dombrowski, *The Early Days of Christian Socialism in America* (New York: Columbia University Press, 1936) 17.

32. Charles H. Hopkins, *The Rise of the Social Gospel in American Protestantism 1865-1915* (New Haven: Yale University Press, 1940) 3.

33. Timothy L. Smith, *Revivalism and Social Reform in Mid-Nineteenth-century America* (New York: Abingdon, 1957) 8.

34. Smith 148.

35. Smith 149.

36. Smith 149.

37. Smith 162.

CHAPTER 4

A Defense of the Faith

*The teachings of philosophy and ethics are cold and unat-
tractive. But the story of Jesus is naturally fitted to win the
hearts and draw all men unto Him. Let us be sure to tell
the story true. The Gospel is not a system of theology, not a
code of morals, not an anathema of judgment, but the
message of one who loved us and gave Himself for us.
(August 3, 1907)*

Conservative evangelical Protestantism in America found
itself under attack from the forces of liberalism at the close
of the nineteenth century. Many defenses of evangelicalism
appeared at the end of the century and early in the twentieth
century as evangelical Christians, soon to be labeled "fundamentalists," strove to protect churches, denominations and
educational institutions from liberalism-modernism.
Throughout the sermons and editorials produced by A.B.
Simpson during that time period there are constant defenses of
orthodoxy and critical analyses of liberal theology. The clearest
gathering of his views on this conflict was published in 1911 in
The Old Faith and the New Gospels.

Simpson presented the theological questions of his day by
juxtaposing the newer ideas to the "old faith" handed down by
preceding generations of orthodox believers. In his statements

on the newer theological ideas, we gain insight into the exposure he had to views being put forth by the religious thinkers of his day. He frequently cited authors and books, at other times he noted only ideas without attaching them to any person or school of thought. After noting the new ideas he would state his conviction on the core truths, which he then confirmed as being consistent with the tradition of previous Christian thinkers. The book is a strong defense of the doctrines Simpson thought to be the most crucial for evangelical believers, who were facing severe testing from "so-called Christians" seeking to undermine evangelical beliefs. His relief-oriented premillennial social theory becomes evident as he questions the liberal-modernist theological innovations of his day.

Simpson used the language of military combat to describe the theological controversies of his day. He stood among those who were prepared to fight to maintain a pure and undefiled faith.

> The present generation has witnessed a simultaneous attack upon the foundations of our faith on half a dozen different lines. The first is directed against the very throne of God Himself, through the teaching of "science, falsely so called," especially the doctrine of Darwinian evolution. The next comes through un-friendly scholarship in the name of Higher Criticism and is directed against the authority, integrity and inspiration of the Holy Scriptures. Another, under the name of New Theology, assails the person, deity, aton-ing work and resurrection of the Lord Jesus Christ. Another, Ethical Culture, offers us a substitute for supernatural religion, regeneration, and Christian ex-perience through the Holy Ghost. Still another would give us Socialism as a substitute for the kingdom and

> coming of the Lord Jesus Christ. Again the battle
> ground is moved to the body, and through the new
> Psychology, Christian Science and other counterfeits,
> the teaching of God's Holy Word concerning divine life
> for the body through redemption is assailed. So from all
> sides the line of battle is leading up to Armageddon and
> sometimes it seems like not far away.[1]

His intention was to arouse like-minded conservative Christians to the need of opposing the new forces and doctrines which he saw working to undermine the very foundations of true Christianity.

Simpson's *The Old Faith and the New Gospels* appeared shortly after the publication of *The Fundamentals*. This collection of essays written by various conservative theologians to counterattack the increasing number of "errors" that were overtaking churches and denominations early in the twentieth century, first appeared as a series of paperback volumes published between 1910 and 1915. Simpson's tone is decidedly "fundamentalist" in nature, although he rightfully belongs to the generation preceding the rise of militant fundamentalism.

A Summary of Simpson

A survey of Simpson's *The Old Faith and the New Gospels* follows:

Evolution or Creation?

Simpson begins by quoting two verses of Scripture in support of divine creation. He then calls attention to Charles Darwin's books *Origin of the Species* and *The Descent of Man* as being the starting point for the evolutionary theory that man has evolved from lower forms of life, with weaker forms

of life perishing through a process of natural selection, ultimately leaving only the surviving fittest forms of life. He
argued that evolutionary thinking had gone far beyond
biological evolution. In the hands of popularizers of Darwinian thought, evolutionary speculation had "led to an attempt to explain everything in the universe, not only in the
world of matter and of nature, but in the world of mind,
morals, society, politics, and even religion, on the principle of
evolution or development." The views expressed by Herbert
Spencer, America's leading Darwinian, were seen by Simpson
as "more serious in their direct bearing along lines of spiritual
truth than as mere scientific explanation of the phenomena of
nature."[2] His argument was not strictly limited to Darwin's
theory as it challenged belief in divine creation, he also saw a
clear danger in the application of Darwin to the social sciences
by Spencer and Social Darwinians. They saw mankind as
progressing toward a higher and better intellectual and social
culture as the "fittest" replaced the "weak" or "unadaptable"
in society. They labeled evangelical/fundamentalist religion as
the "lower," "weaker" religion that was in the process of being
replaced by enlightened Christian liberalism, which would in
turn be replaced by secularism.

Those opposed to Christianity, "agnostics and infidels," wrote
Simpson, claimed evolution as a fatal blow to the validity of
Scripture and supernatural religion. The spread of evolutionary
thought was immediate and pervasive, Simpson noted, from
preachers to public schools to common people: "today a flood
of unbelief is sweeping over Christendom which is largely due
to the perverting influence of much false teaching which is not
only unproved scientifically, but is disproved and denied in all
its extreme forms by the teaching of the Word of God."[3]

Simpson's attack upon evolution was twofold: first to show

that it was unproven scientifically; then to show that it was unscriptural.

In declaring evolution to be scientifically unproven Simpson pointed to Spencer's qualifying remark that the evolutionary theory was only the start of a complex process of scientific research. He also cited an associate of Darwin named Wallace who refused to affirm the claim that the theory accounted for man's intellectual, moral and spiritual development. He pointed to the inability of scientists to cross-breed animals to come up with new species. Finally, he cited Darwin himself who had commented on geologic records which indicated sudden and distinct epochs in nature as evidence that his theory had not been proven.

Other thinkers were enlisted by Simpson to reinforce his argument that God could not be excluded from the creation process. He cited Sir Isaac Newton's assertion, in *Principia*, that the universe must be the product of an intelligent and powerful being; Sir William Thompson's claim that nature has an "intelligent and benevolent design"; Huxley, who remained unconvinced that evolution held all the answers; Tyndalls' statement that science had failed to create life independently; Von Hartmann's conclusion that by 1906 "it had become apparent that the days of Darwinism are numbered"; The London Times' report in 1905 that evolutionists were becoming humorous in their claims and counter claims that they "represent" science; Thomas Edison's statement that, "There are more frauds in science than anywhere else"; Lyall's declaration that at the beginning of the nineteenth century, eighty geological theories opposed the Bible, yet fifty years later none of these theories were validated; and an unnamed living scientist's assertion that new species had not been found to derive from other known species.[4]

When he turned to the defense of biblical creationism Simpson asserted, "The story of creation in the first chapter of Genesis is not contradicted by any established fact of science." In support of this assertion he referred to the Gladstone-Huxley debates, (the celebrated public debates conducted in England). He, of course, sided with Gladstone's position that the order of creation in Genesis was correct and that science agreed with that order.[5] While he saw evolution at odds with the biblical account of creation he allowed for what he labeled the "true place of evolution." He wrote, "There is a place for a modified doctrine of evolution or development as a method by which the great First Cause or Creator accomplishes much of His work, and especially by which He carries on the great processes of nature and providence under His divine supervision." He noted, however, that "this is very different from the extreme doctrine which would exclude a First Cause and Creator at every new stage in the origin of life on this planet."[6]

Simpson's concern was for the spiritual ramifications of the teachings of evolution as well. He pointed to the lives of Darwin and Spencer as examples of men who began as believers and ended up abandoning the Christian religion and even belief in God.[7]

He was distressed about the effects of evolution on philosophy, morals and religion. He noted William James' view that in the universities of Britain and America monotheism was denied while church members continued to verbally confess the "lifeless formula" of an "external Creator." He quoted at length from a Sir Joseph Compton Rickett, a British thinker, who was attempting to apply the doctrine of evolution to God. Rickett wrote, ". . . our heavenly Father is Himself but a product of Evolution, Who has been evolved from a great age of struggle with forces of evil in the universe and Who is necessarily limited by His environment and is not as almighty as professed Christians always supposed." Simpson found such conclusions to be shocking.[8]

Simpson concluded his argument against evolution by attacking the notion of "evolution of character," the "gradual development from latent principles of goodness in human nature," which he found expressed by social evolutionists. "There is no germ in human nature that can develop into grace," wrote Simpson. "There is nothing left but a wreck, so hopeless that it is beyond reconstruction." Regeneration through Jesus Christ, he emphasized, was the only means of making man a "new creation." He continued, "Socialism and modern philosophy are preaching that culture, fine art, modern newspapers, public libraries, better theatre, better politics and higher wages will regenerate society. No, salvation is a crisis, a revolution, a divine creation," He asserted, ". . . the modern church is evolutionizing the millennium," by saying that the millennium was "going to grow out of the trade union, the institutional church, the republican or democratic party, the arbitration treaty, the new humanism. No, no, the City of God, the New Jerusalem, cometh down out of heaven and the new age will burst like a revelation upon an astonished world."[9]

In the final analysis, for Simpson, one must accept the biblical account of creation by faith. Creation was a supernatural event. Simpson held that, "We need continually to believe in a God who can make things out of nothing."[10]

Simpson had little faith in the power of man through science or education to create either new forms of life or a better life on earth. On the other hand, he had great faith in the ability of God to both create and regenerate life.

Higher Criticism and the Authority of the Bible
The type of higher biblical criticism which challenged tradi-

tional views on the authorship, dating and inerrancy of the Bible was opposed by Simpson who wrote:

> It is quite different from the old infidelity which aimed at the destruction of the entire Bible. On the contrary it professes the greatest respect for the Bible and its teachers, likes nothing so well as a pulpit or a professor's chair in a Theological Seminary, but at the same time while sailing under the colors of the Bible is really its most dangerous foe, and the great adversary is fighting his last and best battle against Christianity, not from the outside, but from the inside, with a pirate captain and hostile crew on board the ship of professed Christianity.[11]

This attack upon Scripture was seen by Simpson as the work of Satan. The defense of the Bible was seen as crucial, for "if the Scriptures have lost their absolute authority, they cease to be the infallible Word of God and simply take their place with the human literature of other ages and nations."[12]

Higher criticism was seen by Simpson as embracing the "study of the origins, dates and authorship of the various parts of the Bible, the literary structure of the different books which make up the great library of the sacred volume." He saw this criticism as an assault upon the authority of the Bible from those who wanted to "eliminate everything supernatural" from the God's Word.[13]

Starting with the attacks on the Mosaic authorship of the Pentateuch made by Spinoza, Hobbes and Astruc, Simpson traced the increased level of challenges to the authority of the Bible. He named a long line of higher critics in Germany, England and America. "Ewald, Kuenan, Bauer, Wellhausen, Colenso,

Robertson Smith, George Adam Smith, Prof. Cheyne, Dr. Driver and Dr. Briggs" were listed as rationalists who did not believe in miracles, prophecy, revelation or anything supernatural.[14]

Simpson defended Scripture by appealing to the Bible's internal argument for inspiration and validity coupled with an appeal to the argument from experience. "We know it is true because it has been true to us. We know it is inspired because it has inspired our hearts and transformed our lives."[15] He asserted, "When you cannot see the Bible clearly with your intellect take it to your heart and the Holy Ghost will make it to you the very life of Jesus."[16]

Just as his defense of the biblical account of creation centered on an appeal to faith, so also Simpson's strongest defense of the authority of the Bible was an appeal to faith. In a day when science and the scientific method were becoming the authority for mankind, Simpson could not offer empirical evidence for the validity of the Scriptures. Ultimately one must accept by faith that the Bible is the Word of God, true and steadfast despite the opposition of certain scholars and scientists.

The New Theology and Jesus Christ

The "New Theology" spoken of by Simpson was represented in his mind by one theologian in particular, Reginald Campbell of Great Britain. Simpson summed up the "New Theology" as belief in divine immanence the "natural identity of God with man, which is very difficult to separate from the doctrine of Pantheism." He quoted Campbell, "Humanity is divinity viewed from below; divinity is humanity viewed from above."[17] Simpson saw this as resulting in a view of man as "a light and law to himself" with the Bible having no authority over mankind. "New Theology" asserted that, "all men are the children of God naturally." He found this notion of the Fatherhood of God to be common to all forms of "New Theology" and to Socialism as well. Both found it to be beneficial, he charged, since it did away with "repentance, conversion and a supernatural change of heart,"[18] The "New Theology," as Simpson saw it, posited that there was no sin or punishment for sin, that salvation was to be found by ceasing to be selfish and, instead, living a life of self-sacrifice and love.[19]

Simpson wrote of the "New Theology" that Jesus becomes only human, "a man, a typical man, a perfect man but only a man."[20] The atonement and the cross "cease to be a divine provision for human salvation and becomes a human imitation of divine sacrifice and love. We become our own saviours and in turn the saviours of others." The resurrection becomes a purely spiritual event, not a literal physical resurrection. Simpson wrote, "Of course, regeneration, sanctification and everything connected with a supernatural life, such as prayer, must go in this great sweep of mere humanism."[21]

Simpson's final quote from Campbell on the New Theology contains the core of what Simpson found to be objectionable in this new approach to Christian doctrine. "The moment we succeed in disentangling ourselves from all literal and limiting New Testament statements about the connection between sin and physical death, the physical resurrection, the distant judgment day, and such like," Campbell wrote, "we find ourselves in a position to appreciate the beautiful experience in which these very terms become symbols of inner realities of the soul." Simpson objected to this most strongly because it sought to eliminate the foundational truths of the New Testament. Campbell espoused a view of salvation that differed from traditional evangelical theology. "The only salvation we need trouble about is the changing of selfishness to love," Campbell wrote. "Heaven and hell are states of the soul." He added, "The object of salvation is not the getting of man into heaven, but the getting of heaven into him."[22]

This New Theology, presented by Reginald Campbell, Simpson labeled "another gospel." He refused to recognize it as in any way consistent with the orthodox faith and doctrine found in the Bible and called it anathema.

Ethical Culture and the Christ Life

There were some in Simpson's day who talked of the perfectibility of man and society through the cultivation of character. They believed that man could, if properly nourished and educated, live a selfless life of love and brotherhood. Groups were begun calling themselves Ethical Culture to foster altruistic love and universal harmony. They optimistically believed, along with social gospel theologians, that man was progressing toward a better and more perfect society every day. All that was needed was recognition that man could indeed live a selfless loving life of peace with his neighbor.

Simpson found Ethical Culture to be a deficient way of dealing with the problems of human society and the human soul. "Human nature alone is unable to rise even to its own ideals. It needs higher ideals, but even those are beyond its reach. It is the old homey figure of a man trying to lift himself into the air by his boot straps," wrote Simpson. "He needs a power outside of himself to lift him above the human plane."[23] He quoted Tolstoy, who said, "Man needs no atonement, no sacrifice, no redeeming blood. All that he requires is the Sermon on the Mount and an honest living up to it." To which Simpson replied, "But the Sermon on the Mount is not the Gospel and never has saved and never will save a human soul."[24]

In the place of Ethical Culture, Simpson offered the regenerative power of life in Jesus Christ. He noted, "It is the love of

Christ that comes through the acceptance of His redeeming grace that provides the motive power for holy character." To those who sought to walk in the footsteps of Jesus he wrote, "I need Jesus of Nazareth Himself within me to walk in His footsteps." What was needed, he added, was "a new creation, a new nature, a new heart." Regeneration alone, however, would not suffice because the old human nature would continue to be at war with the new nature. The believer needed to be indwelt by the Holy Spirit in order to have the Christ-life produced in his or her life. Anything short of regeneration and sanctification, according to Simpson, would fail, for "in the pride of human self-righteousness they are going about to establish their own righteousness and have not submitted themselves to the righteousness of God."[25]

Divine Healing and Its Counterfeits

"God has given a high place to the human body in the plan of redemption," asserted A.B. Simpson, a firm believer in the ability of the human body to be healed by God. This gift of God to believers stemmed from the atoning work of Christ, who was crucified so that bodies as well as souls might be redeemed.[26]

Simpson attacked the "counterfeit" methods of healing that he saw at work in spiritism, Christian Science and the followers of Emmanuel Swedenborg and defended his own belief in divine healing.

While allowing for the use of medicine and medical doctors to aid in healing, all of which were seen as being divine in origin, Simpson made the following statements on divine healing: 1) "Divine healing is not a human method of professional healing, but a simple ministry of the Gospel." 2) "It is not limited to any class of diseases." 3) "It does not demand healing from God presumptuously, but seeks to be humbly subject to His will."

4) "It recognizes the place of chastening and discipline, and holds that chastening is for a definite purpose." 5) "It stems from the redemptive work of the cross." 6) Healing comes through the Holy Spirit. 7) "It requires faith on the part of the subject and simply meets and shares it." 8) It is subordinate to the salvation of souls and the sanctification and consecration of believers.[27]

Socialism and the Kingdom and Coming of Christ

Simpson made his position clear, "The hope of the Church and the Christian is the coming of our Lord and Saviour Jesus Christ and the kingdom which He is to set up on this blighted and misgoverned world." He surveyed world history and found that the "god of this world" was seeking to set up a counterfeit kingdom. The falling of monarchies and the rise in democracy convinced Simpson that the last days were near. He pointed to the rise of populism, socialism and humanism as proof that society was coming apart at the seams.[28]

"Modern socialism and religious apostasy," wrote Simpson, "are joining hands." He gave as evidence Reginald Campbell's statement that, "The great Social movement, which is now taking place in every country of the civilized world toward universal peace and brotherhood, and a better and fairer distribution of wealth, is really the same movement as that which in the more distinctively religious sphere is coming to be called the New Theology. The New Theology is but the religious articulation of the Social movement."[29] Campbell is further quoted, "The great Labor movement, which perhaps more than any other represents the social application of the Christian ideal, should not be out of touch with organized religion. In fact the Labor party is itself a church in the sense in which the word was originally used, for it represents the getting together of those who want to bring about the kingdom of God."[30] Simpson warned that "Christian leaders are easily drawn into this current and so-called Christian Socialism has a powerful organized following in the name of the churches."[31]

Socialism was viewed by Simpson as "unchristian." He quoted what he called the "creed of Socialism" from an unidentified socialist writer named French: ". . . a god of love, a religion of humanity, the brotherhood of all men, the Trinity of love, justice and truth, that capital is the creation of labor and is the property of its creator, that socialism is the gospel of atonement of humanity, for man's inhumanity. Socialism is the second coming of the Elder Brother."[32]

Simpson pointed out some of the atheistic pronouncements of socialist writers. Karl Marx: "The idea of God must be destroyed, it is the keystone of a perverted civilization." Herr Bebel: "The revolution differs from all its predecessors in this, that it does not seek new forms of religion, but denies religion altogether." Belfor Bax: "In what sense Socialism is not a religion will now be clear. It utterly despises 'the other world' with all its stage properties, that is, the present objects of religion. . . . it brings back religion from heaven to earth." Blatchford: "You are infidels who call yourselves Christians. Are you aware that the Socialist, be he a believer or an atheist, is nearer to the Christ you profess to serve than you are yourselves? Are you aware that you cannot deny Socialism without denying Christ?"[33]

Simpson used these direct statements to show that Christianity and socialism were not compatible. He saw socialism as a great enemy of Christianity, out to destroy it by replacing its role in society.

Simpson labeled the modern church belief in the ability of man to bring about the kingdom of God on earth "post-millennialism." He wrote, "Modern Protestants are really expecting no other millennium and no higher manifestation of the kingdom of God on earth than which is to come about through civilization, the spread of the Gospel and the progress of Christianity among the nations."[34] Calling this a "false dream" held by the social gospel movement, social reformers and the "post-millennialist" church, Simpson pointed out the short-comings of such wrong-headed thinking and challenged their position.

> They hail the advent of modern progress, the forces of electricity, steam, radium, the wireless, telegraph, the automobile, the aeroplane, the printing-press, the university, the popular library, the progress of our time as the beginning of the Golden Age. . . . if we for a moment point our fingers to the awful conditions that exist, the poverty, the crime, the cruelty, the luxury, the licentiousness, the lust, the oppression, the Sabbath breaking, the drunkenness, the increase of disorder and crime, and the fact that we have two hundred million more heathen in the world than we had a century ago they call us pessimists and charge us with holding back the chariot of the Lord by the dead weight of our narrowness and conservatism.[35]

Simpson made his own position clear. "The Word of God," he wrote, "gives no sanction to this vain hope of an earthly millennium apart from the coming of Christ Himself." Rather than conditions on earth improving, he argued that things would become steadily worse. There would be a moral and spiritual decline prior to the return of Christ.[36] He put forth a two-stage return of Christ. Stage one, the Parousia, at which time Christ will rapture His church, and stage two, after a season of tribulation, when Christ would return to set up his kingdom for a thousand years.[37]

Practical Conclusions

A final series of warnings were issued by Simpson in the last chapter of *The Old Faith and the New Gospels*. He gave advice to Christians on how to live in what he believed to be the last days.

The tone of his warnings emphasize the fervency of his belief that the end of time was near. He saw clear signs of the approaching end in both politics and commerce. "The political world," he wrote, "is in a similar condition of upheaval and Democracy and Populism are undermining the foundations of every earthly throne. The industrial and commercial world has discovered new forces and new methods which are steadily banishing individual enterprise for larger combinations of trade and commerce." He gave as examples of social ferment the uncertainty of the role of women in society, the instability of the family and the progress of radical socialism as applied to education.[38] Fearing that the very "foundations of society, morals and practical life are being destroyed," Simpson attacked what he called the "religion of Humanity" which he saw as a "system of Socialism that would do away with government, property, and in some cases even family life." He saw it as a "religion" in which, "Morals are to be regulated not by any divine law of purity, but by the common good. . . . Wealth is to be fairly divided and the 'lazy-loafer' is to draw his dividend equally with the 'bloated bondholder.' . . . Of course, the Millennium is to follow."[39]

What should Christian believers do in the face of these new religious ideas? Simpson advised, "Let us make sure of our own foundations. Let us hold no easy, cheap or mere traditional views of sacred things. Let us search the Scriptures. . . . Mere second hand beliefs will be swept away in the fierce stream."[40] He cautioned the faithful, "Do not try to take the middle ground of compromise, accepting the conclusion of Higher Criticism and yet holding on to the fragments of faith that are left. . . . The Bible must be wholly true or a rope of sand. Christ must be everything or nothing."[41]

Education was an area of great concern to Simpson. Basing his conclusion, in part, on some statements made by the philosopher William James, Simpson argued that the colleges and universities of America and Britain were teaching a philosophy "which necessarily destroys all the foundations of belief in a personal God, infinite, eternal and wholly separate from and immeasurably above His creation."[42] He proposed an alternative means of education: "the time has come when Christian schools, high schools and colleges, recognizing the authority of the Bible and the Lord Jesus and hallowed by a spiritual atmosphere are an absolute necessity for the families of the children of God."[43]

World missions was another area that Simpson felt was in danger of being contaminated by modernism. "Liberal thought on the mission fields has at length begun to trifle with that which is good, so-called, in the religions of the East, an unholy alliance which God forbids." He asserted the need to present an undiluted Christian message of personal sin and repentance.[44]

We have seen the clear message of Simpson that there could be no moves toward compromising evangelical Christian faith with the New Theology. He saw the hope of an earthly millennium apart from the physical return of Christ as a false belief. He strongly reaffirmed the authority of the Bible and a thoroughly biblical faith, not just because of tradition, but because this faith remained the true faith.

Simpson called on Christians to rebuild their fortresses to face the impending battle. "Beloved, the foundations are being destroyed. What shall the righteous do?" He challenged, "Let them fly to the breaches, let them become repairers of the wasted places, the restorers of paths to dwell in. Let them stand in the old paths and the good way. Let them be wise master builders whose work will stand when the wood, hay and stubble of all our modernism shall drift away in the flames of a dissolving world."[45]

Endnotes

1. A.B. Simpson, *The Old Faith and the New Gospels* (New York: Christian Alliance Publishing Co., 1911) 7-8.
2. Simpson *Faith* 10.
3. Simpson *Faith* 11.
4. Simpson *Faith* 13-18.
5. Simpson *Faith* 19.
6. Simpson *Faith* 11-12.
7. Simpson *Faith* 21-23.
8. Simpson *Faith* 24.
9. Simpson *Faith* 27-28, (also see Simpson, "Thy Kingdom Come," *The Alliance Weekly*, 24 Oct. 1914: 51 and Simpson, "The Significance of Our Times," *The Christian Alliance*, 19 Oct. 1894: 372-373).
10. Simpson *Faith* 28-29.
11. Simpson *Faith* 30-31
12. Simpson *Faith* 32.
13. Simpson *Faith* 32-33.
14. Simpson *Faith* 34.
15. Simpson *Faith* 55.
16. Simpson *Faith* 57.
17. Simpson *Faith* 59.

18. Simpson *Faith* 63.
19. Simpson *Faith* 66-73.
20. Simpson *Faith* 73.
21. Simpson *Faith* 78.
22. Simpson *Faith* 78-79.
23. Simpson *Faith* 82-83.
24. Simpson *Faith* 89.
25. Simpson *Faith* 90-92, (also see Simpson, "Our Trust," *The Christian and Missionary Alliance*, 28 May 1910: 145-146).
26. Simpson *Faith* 100.
27. Simpson *Faith* 115-118.
28. Simpson *Faith* 119-121.
29. Simpson *Faith* 123.
30. Simpson *Faith* 124.
31. Simpson *Faith* 127.
32. Simpson *Faith* 128-129.
33. Simpson *Faith* 129-130.
34. Simpson *Faith* 134.
35. Simpson *Faith* 134.
36. Simpson *Faith* 136, (also see Simpson, *The Coming One* New York: Christian Alliance Publishing Co., 1912, 226-227).
37. Simpson *Faith* 137.
38. Simpson *Faith* 143.
39. Simpson *Faith* 148-149.
40. Simpson *Faith* 152.
41. Simpson *Faith* 154.
42. Simpson *Faith* 144-145.
43. Simpson *Faith* 157.
44. Simpson *Faith* 159-160.
45. Simpson *Faith* 161.

CHAPTER 5

Social Activities Resulting from Simpson's Ministry

. . . the Church of God has not yet more than begun to realize all that tact can do to win them; all that sympathy and consideration for their distress can do to awaken their confidence; and above everything, all that faith can do to bring to bear upon them the constraining, power and love of God. All this is implied, and a little of it is illustrated in the Christian philanthropies and blessed agencies of consecrated evangelism in our own and other days; and it is sufficiently vindicated, and proved effectual from the fact that multitudes of the most honored servants of God, and even the ministers of the Gospel of Jesus Christ, have been snatched from these very ranks; rescued from the very gates of hell; emancipated from the spiritual and literal prisons and chains; pulled out of the seething pollutions of prostitution; and saved from the gambling saloon, and barroom, and pick-pockets' den, to leave behind them the glorious record of a Bunyan, a Newton, or a Jerry McAuley. (December 23, 1905)

When A.B. Simpson arrived in New York City in 1879 to pastor the fashionable Thirteenth Street Church and to launch his illustrated missionary magazine, *The Gospel in All*

Lands, he entered a city in the midst of great economic, industrial and population expansion. New York was the port of entry for numerous waves of immigration. Many European immigrants settled in the city, while others moved on to settle in other parts of the land of opportunity. They provided much of the work force for the rapidly industrialized America of the post-Civil War period. Soon many other east coast cities would share the acute problems faced by New York: slum housing conditions, disease, poor working conditions and obstacles to education for the masses. Immigration coupled with migration from rural America into the cities fostered many social problems in the late nineteenth century.

Henry F. May gives a glimpse of cities, and of New York in particular, at the end of the nineteenth century, in his book *Protestant Churches and Industrial America*. "As the cities became centers of progress in the arts, sciences, business, industry and philanthropy, they developed also as breeding grounds of poverty, misery, vice and crime. In the contrast between Fifth Avenue and the disease-ridden Lower East Side, class gulfs were dramatized as never before in America."[1]

A writer in that period, Charles Stetzle, wrote the following description in *A Son of the Bowery*:

> The filthy slum, the dark tenement, the unsanitary factory, the long hours of toil, the lack of living wage, the back breaking labor, the inability to pay doctor's bills in times of sickness, the poor and insufficient food, the lack of leisure, the swift approach of old age, the dismal future,—these weighted down the hearts and lives of multitudes in our cities. Many have almost forgotten how to smile. To laugh is a lost art. The look of care has come that is now forever stamped upon their

> faces. Lines are deep and hard; their souls—their ethical souls—are all but lost. No hell in the future can be worse to them than the hell in which they now live.[2]

Fresh from successful evangelistic efforts in Louisville, Simpson came to New York City with a vision to reach the unchurched with the gospel message both at home and abroad. He enjoyed success evangelizing immigrants while pastoring Thirteenth Street Church and he envisioned an even larger ministry to the poorer classes in New York before he left the Presbyterian Church to begin his independent work.

Simpson relinquished control and the editorship of *The Gospel in All Lands*, his first missionary magazine, in 1881 and in 1882, after his break with Thirteenth Street Church, he began *The Word, Work and World.* This was a monthly missions magazine which also contained sermons and articles on evangelizing the home field. It urged churches to reach out to the poor and needy of America's cities.

Simpson addressed himself to the problem of "How the Church Can Reach the Masses" in the very first issue of *The Word, Work and World.* He advocated love as the controlling principle behind all efforts to reach out to the poor. "A church that wants the poor, misses them, seeks them, will always find them, feed them and be filled with them. But," he asked, "Do our churches want them?" He questioned whether churches that gave money to support foreign mission efforts really wanted the poor in their own churches. He argued that churches must adopt methods to attract the masses and, above all things, must abolish pew rents. He also presented the need for evangelistic services, in addition to services for the edification of the saints.[3]

A Church for All Classes

Simpson, in the same first issue of *The Word, Work and World*, urged that "The Rich and the Poor Meet Together." He pointed out the tendency of the churches in large cities to be divided into two classes: affluent churches for the wealthy and mission churches for the poor. He sympathized with the masses of in-between people who might feel unwelcome in fashionable churches and slighted at being consigned to mission churches and who, therefore, were not attending church at all. Their Sundays were increasingly being devoted, according to Simpson, to picnics, outings, parties and other recreational activities.[4]

"The Religious Wants of New York," written by Simpson, also in that first issue of *The Word, Work and World*, surveyed religious activities in New York: these included mission churches, asylums, temperance work, industrial training schools, orphanages and other charitable efforts. He concluded, "There is no real progress in numerical results commensurate with the growth of the city." The needs were far outweighing the measures being taken by the churches to meet the needs.

Simpson castigated the pulpits from which "unhallowed worldliness" was being preached and churches where members were "riding to heaven in Palace sleeping cars" while souls were perishing. Churches were moving out of lower class neighborhoods and "concentrating in the wealthy and fashionable districts" uptown, while the poor masses in Lower Manhattan went unchurched. The middle class working people coming into the cities to find jobs were leaving their religion behind in the country because they were shut out of fancy churches. The churches of New York, in Simpson's opinion, were too busy lounging in the sunlight of their luxury and building walls between themselves and the poorer working classes. He bemoaned, "Ah, the Church is losing the poor." The remedy, he felt, was repentance for past mistakes, a baptism in the power of the Holy Spirit and a revival of evangelistic work on the part of Christian churches. He charged, "Let Christians then awake from their respectability. Let religion cease to be an amusement, and let it become a holy trust. Let the churches open their doors freely to all classes."[5]

Two months later, in an editorial, Simpson commented on the gulf between classes in America's churches: "But it seems to be reserved for republican Americans to present to the world a spectacle in the church of God which finds its only precedent in the castes of India or the clubs of worldly society."[6]

There is evidence that Simpson began to formulate ideas about what the churches should be doing to break down class distinctions before his arrival in New York. Thompson's biography tells of his position on church and society while in Louisville. The church "must be free, free in the full sense that all shall give gladly, freely to God according to their means, the cents of the poor being as welcome as the thousands of the rich, and no man excluded because the rich can pay $100 per year for a pew." Simpson also made efforts to visit the poverty-stricken, neglected areas on the outskirts of Louisville and was touched by what he saw.[7] It can definitely be said, whether while still in Louisville or early in his pastorate in New York, that Simpson was opposed to pew rent and made efforts to bring the unchurched poor into the church.

Right from the outset of his independent work, reaching the poor, unreached throngs of New York's lower classes was a high priority for Simpson. Thompson discusses the various activities and programs designed to meet the needs of the poor. Of the early beginnings of The Christian and Missionary Alliance, he wrote, "Though the movement was not a rescue mission, special efforts were made from the very beginning to reach the submerged element in the city, and such missions in New York and elsewhere look to the Alliance for warmest sympathy and support."[8] The last day of each New York missionary convention of The Christian and Missionary Alliance was devoted to rescue mission work.

Thompson details the rescue mission work which were begun or conducted by Simpson and his associates in New York City and vicinity:

Simpson's Efforts

In 1885 two missions were opened, one on Thirteenth Street near Greenwich, the other, known as Berachah Mission, on Twenty-ninth Street near Ninth Avenue. Later a new Berachah Mission was erected at Tenth Avenue and West Thirty-second Street which, at the time, was "the best equipped mission in the city," with work among sailors and a free medical dispensary for the poor of the neighborhood. In 1899 another mission was opened on Eleventh Avenue near Thirty-eighth Street, known as the Eleventh Street Mission. Thompson noted, "As one of the earliest developments a service was opened in 1882 at 120 West Twenty-seventh Street for the salvation of the fallen women who crowded that part of the city." In 1891 "The Door of Hope" mission was opened to rescue girls. Although it was an independent work, unaffiliated with the Gospel Tabernacle, it had the cooperation and aid of Simpson and his church. The South Street Mission was started by the ladies of Simpson's church and The Colby Mission in Greenpoint Brooklyn by one of Simpson's students. The Eighth Avenue Mission was opened by Miss May Agnew, the organizational secretary of The Christian and Missionary Alliance in 1899. Berachah Orphanage was opened in the summer of 1886. First located at 329 East Fiftieth Street, it was later moved to College Point, Long Island and finally to Nyack, New York.[9]

Beyond these works, Pardington noted, "In addition to the associated departments and auxiliary agencies of the church, the consecrated energies of the members, particularly of the young people, have been directed to holding open air meetings, services in jails, hospitals, on shipboard in the harbor, and in many other places. . . ."[10]

A.E. Funk, one of Simpson's associates, gave this rationale for these works: "The homes and institutions of the Alliance were pressed into existence by the needs which they now, in part at least, meet in many places, rather than opened by selfish desires and purposes and then begging for patronage."[11] Simpson and his followers saw acute needs and acted to relieve them. He worried about finances later.

Although much of the work was of direct spiritual activity, physical as well as spiritual needs were met. The Ladies Aid Society of the Gospel Tabernacle had an active program in poor neighborhoods. It was reported that, "Many of the ladies visit regularly the tenement and other houses in the district, distributing cards of invitation and tracts and speaking of Christ to the inmates. They also have committees on charitable relief, employment and care of the sick."[12]

Simpson's Support

Simpson was not always directly involved in the daily operation of gospel welfare work carried on by Alliance workers, but, as leader of the movement, he was responsible for the general supervision of the work. As he toured the country on evangelistic tours he visited the rescue works and reported on them in his magazines. He was most often in touch with the work carried on in New York City and vicinity. The people conducting the work received his blessing and inspiration since many of them were members of his church. The pages of Simpson's magazines appear to have been open to reports from other rescue mission and gospel welfare activities outside of the Alliance. Funds for these works were solicited in that manner.

The Word, Work and World became a place where other writers could cry out against the church's inaction in social concerns. Mrs. Henry Naylor, reporting on the "Midnight Mission" on Twenty-seventh Street in New York, vigorously argued that churches were helping only the rich and were ignoring the poor. She labeled them failures for not reaching the masses. "Jesus wants souls, not comfortable churches;" she wrote, "homes, not cushioned pews; not artistic music, but sturdy hand-to-hand fight with the enemy of souls in his very lair." She believed that churches would be held accountable for not reaching the "poor, hungry masses." She forcefully argued:

> Shall the theatres, drinking saloons and houses of pros-
> titution, made attractive with brilliant lights and soul
> moving music through their doors, open every night to
> draw in the idle and thoughtless, and help them on to
> eternal death, and we, the followers of Jesus, do nothing
> to counteract this hellish work of the Evil One? But hold
> a preaching service of two sermons on Sunday in chur-
> ches monopolized by the sleepers, and one feeble prayer
> meeting during the week? Ah, friend, there is danger!
> When we come to the end we may hear the Master say,
> "Depart, I know you not." "I was hungered and ye gave
> me no meat. Inasmuch as you did not unto them you
> did it not unto me."[13]

Hephzibah House and Training School for Christian Workers was opened in December of 1893, on West 56th Street. It was to "provide a school where working girls, who have not had the advantages of early education and wish to consecrate their lives to Christian work, can receive instruction in the Bible, be thoroughly grounded in the common English branches, together with industrial training, and experimental Christian work." Classes were also held in millinery, dress-making, physical culture, embroidery, stenography and household economy.[14]

One rescue mission report, a non-Alliance work, in *The Word, Work and World*, told of the dangerous street where the mission was located but how, through the activities of the mission, the street had now been made safe with some of the saloons even closing down.[15]

Charles Gibbord described his Florence Mission, on Bleecker Street, in November of 1885. "We provide a refuge . . . for any fallen woman who wants to stay a while until she can find a better home." He noted, "We try and bring them into temporary refuge, and then to Christ the eternal refuge."[16]

After attending the first National Convention of Christian Workers in Chicago in June of 1886, where 600 Christian workers discussed work among the poor, neglected and needy, Mrs. Naylor submitted a full report which was published in *The Word, Work and World* detailing the rescue mission work being done in the United States, Canada and England. She also presented the needs of poor women and children, temperance and the need for better prisons.[17]

A report about the deplorable life of fallen women in New York City, published in the second issue of *The Word, Work and World*, asked that homes be established to get the women off the street and rehabilitate them. It reported:

There are today on the streets of New York and in the dens of vice and shame many who were once hard working girls that struggled and struggled against the tempting gold of their employers, until at last, in a weak moment, they gave way, and she was left a hapless, friendless outcast, with no human eye to pity, and no strong arm to save. Alas, poor sister, many are thy accusers, while he laughs and enjoys the society of his family and even takes the uppermost seats in the synagogue.[18]

The rescue mission work discussed at meetings in conjunction with conventions in Simpson's Gospel Tabernacle were often presented to a larger audience in magazine articles. "Reports of Christian Work" in 1886 covered the ministries of the Water Street, Cremorne, Bible and Fruit, Florence, Berachah and Howard missions. It detailed their work in feeding, clothing, finding employment and preaching to the poor.[19] The Bowery Mission and its facilities were described in 1887. The mission had three upper stories which provided temporary housing for 60-70 men, a library and a bathing room.[20]

The Woman's Branch of City Mission provided medical assistance as well as spiritual aid. A medical missionary made rounds in the community "as a ministering angel, giving proper remedies and food, often having to clean the room with her own hands, and having done what she could for one sufferer, go on to another," after which there would usually be an opening for Christian witness.[21]

A report from an 1894 convention at Old Orchard Beach, Maine, told of work being conducted in New York City and Syracuse. "Dr. Furry of New York, gave an account of the outside work in New York City, in the hospitals, almshouses and charitable institutions, and said he did not believe even Mr. Simpson knew how much the Alliance was doing for all the agencies of Christian work in New York City."[22]

The New York convention in the autumn of 1895 is another example of the work the Alliance and other evangelical organizations were doing to reach the needy. Reports on The Bowery, Church, Florence Missions and the Home for Intemperate Men missions; work among the police; work among poverty-stricken blacks in South Carolina, Georgia and Florida; and the Alliance orphanage in New York chronicled the efforts being made to reach the poor and minister to their needs.[23]

The openness of the Alliance to support and work with other groups involved in rescue mission work is recorded in the annual report of The Christian and Missionary Alliance for the year 1895. "Many of the Rescue Missions either established by or in connection with the Alliance are still in active operation," it is reported. "There are scores of rescue bands and workers who have received great spiritual help and sympathy from Alliance people.[24]

The charitable work being carried out in New York City by all types of evangelical groups was presented by Simpson in the editorial "The Dark and Bright Side of Christmas." He wrote, "One would be surprised to find the immense provision which is made for the relief of the suffering and the temporal and spiritual help of the needy." To which he added, "Thank God for the love and thought and care which are providing for the suffering and sin around us here. May God multiply the blessing until it shall reach the greater need of all the world." Along with this editorial there appeared a picture of the building housing the Charity Organization Society, with a note of praise for its work.[25]

Simpson served on the board of trustees of the Steele Home

for Needy Children in Chattanooga, Tennessee. Mrs. A.S. Steele presented the work to Alliance readers in *The Christian Alliance* in 1895. She told of the great need of black children for a home and school in an area where they were prohibited regular state and municipal facilities for orphans. Starting in 1884, she had already trained nearly 500 children in religion, grammar and practical skills. A visitation program to hospitals, jails and poorhouses was also being conducted. She wrote, "Mr. Simpson is Vice-president of our board of trustees, and several of his students from the Institute have been helpers in our home."[26]

Simpson spoke at the dedication of a mission in Astoria, Long Island in 1897. The work was under the leadership of one of his former students. The address was published in the Alliance magazine so that supplies and funds could be channeled to it.[27]

A work being conducted in Williamsport, Pennsylvania among drunks, gamblers and harlots was reported on in 1897. Efforts there were being made to reach "down and lift up the very lowest, those for whom no man cared."[28]

A significant Alliance rescue work was conducted in Denver during the 1890s. It was reported that, "An employment bureau, a medical dispensary and a second-hand clothes room," " a restaurant, where five-cent meals were served" and "a lodging house" had been established, and that "A home was established to care for the women rescued from lives of shame."[29]

A Compassion for Individuals

A compassion for the needs of individuals comes across in the published reports of all these activities. Henry Wilson wrote of the Magdalen Home, "Every woman and girl has a history. From almost every grade of life and social position they have come to this home for rest and deliverance. . . . Some have gone on long in the dark and sad way; others just begun."[30] Mrs. O.S.

Schultz wrote of the work at Berachah Orphanage, "I wish you could all know how blessed children's work is. To do for them that have nothing, the fatherless orphans, the destitute widows and strangers. It brings us all kinds of opportunities to help and do good, to feed the hungry, clothe the naked, to help the needy."[31] A few months later she wrote, "Many a time we could only weep with the mothers who, when all failed, have brought their children to us, and the heart-strings of mother to children had to be broken. We have seen children weep until they could weep no more, and all we could say or do was to comfort them and weep with them."[32] Another article about the orphanage added, "Christian love should complete the full circle and while ministering to the salvation of the perishing world we should not forget to feed His little lambs."[33]

S.H. Hadley reporting on rescue mission work in 1896 wrote, "It means far more to save a drunkard than merely to save a human soul, not omitting to place the priceless value on a human soul but to see a man who has been known for years to be drunken, and worthless, go about clothed and in his right mind, a clean, sweet Christian, oh! it is the loudest kind of sermon!"[34]

The spiritual and the physical needs of people were being met. J.G.H. Simpson told, in his report on the 31st anniversary of the Water Street Mission, of the "rebuilding of wrecked lives through the simple Gospel of Christ." He reported also that, "There was given away during the year to help penniless men, 40,560 nights lodging and 54,000 meals; . . . . Added to this are the many gifts of clothing, shoes and help of other nature to enable men to start to help themselves."[35]

The breadth of Alliance involvement in rescue mission work, both its own and of other organizations, was highlighted in an article by Miss M. Agnew in 1901. She reported, "A large number of Rescue Missions in New York and other cities are in direct touch with the Alliance." She told of missions in Philadelphia, Scranton, Williamsport, Pittsburgh and Chicago with "close affiliation with the Alliance," which had been conducting "productive" rescue work.[36]

Simpson noted in his annual report for 1908: "Rescue missions are carried on in Nyack, New York, Philadelphia, Pittsburgh, Toronto, and indeed, in many other places in direct connection with our regular work and in scores of other places our Alliance people will be found among the leading workers in independent rescue missions which form so important a part of the religious life of our land today."[37]

During the early 1890s virtually every issue of Simpson's magazines carried a column on temperance which generally observed the increase in liquor consumption or the devastating effects of drunkenness.

Simpson's Concern for African-Americans

The Alliance carried on a work among African-Americans. Simpson, in an editorial written in 1898, stated, "One of the most unique and encouraging features of the Alliance work in Ohio and Pennsylvania is the successful organization of a number of strong branches of our beloved colored brethren." He noted, "they are . . . attracted to the heart-stirring truths and deep spirituality of the Alliance movement."[38]

A report on the Third Annual Convention of African-American workers in Pittsburgh in 1898, written by E.B. Nichols, noted that, "The interest increased steadily, and we believe there has been great and effectual work accomplished by our Father through this branch of the Christian and Missionary Alliance among the colored people, who, because of past oppression, . . . will not press their way into conventions where these truths are taught. . . ." He also reported on efforts being undertaken to extend work into the South.[39]

The Alliance work among African-Americans apparently began in the early 1890s. "A Sketch of the Work Being Done in Ohio," written by Mattie A. Bowles in 1898, recorded that, "Six years ago a little humble work began in my home." Along with her helper, Sister Smoot, Bowles visited house to house for a year, and then began meetings in a "private home in one of the lowest streets in Cleveland. The Lord did a great work there, and led us in that room to organize into a Christian Alliance band, September 8, 1895."[40]

Simpson reported in 1899 that, "Much excellent work is being done among our colored brethren in various parts of the country. Some of our best Alliance branches in Ohio and Pennsylvania are exclusively among them and are supporting several missionaries."[41]

The Annual Report of The Christian and Missionary Alliance for 1910-1911 contained a report by E.M. Collett on meetings held for African-Americans in Lenoir, Greensboro, Lovejoy, Ayr and Ashville, North Carolina; Pittsburgh, Philadelphia and Homestead, Pennsylvania; and a "great new tabernacle" built in Winston-Salem, North Carolina.[42]

The Alliance was given control of a Bible school for African-American students in Boydton, Virginia in 1909. This work had been started after the Civil War by Dr. Cullis of Boston and his co-workers.[43] The Alliance annual reports of 1909-1910 and 1911-1912 mention schools for the training of African-American Christian workers. "We thank God for the report of the Lovejoy Missionary Institute and the Mary B. Mullen School relative to progress made during the past year." The report continued, "We would suggest that something more be done than is at present to interest the colored people generally in Lovejoy Institute with a

view to sending them to Africa as missionaries."[44] The 1911-1912
report noted, "We would express much gratitude to God for
continued growth and blessing in our southern schools for
colored students, the Boydton Institute at Boydton, Va., and the
Mary B. Mullen School, at Ayr, N.C."[45]

The Endorsement of Others

One of the strongest endorsements of work among the needy
came from Rev. W.S. Rainsford, pastor of St. George's Episcopal
Church in New York City, where Henry Wilson, one of
Simpson's close associates, was assistant pastor. In a message
originally given at the 23rd Street Tabernacle, at a convention
in 1885, very early in the history of Simpson's independent
work, Rainsford presented the need for work among the poor.
This message sums up the spirit and thrust of the work described
above. Rainsford asserted that work among the masses "must
minister to soul and body if it would be effectual." He added,
"You cannot present the gospel to a hungry man with any hope
of success until you have ministered to his physical wants." He
urged Christian workers to go to the masses as Christ did and
to "Make the poor feel that you care for them, and that His life
has given you new views of life and duty."[46]

The work inspired by Simpson's ministry and the work
directly carried out by agencies of organizations he founded was
a self-less, Christ-centered, concerned outreach to those elements of society that were being overlooked by most churches.
The record shows both an intense desire to save souls and a
desire to see the physical needs of poor, destitute individuals
met, the essence of relief-oriented premillennial social theory.
The ministry was dual in its activities, yet single in its goal, that
men and women should come into a living relationship with
God through Jesus Christ.

Endnotes

1. Henry F. May, *Protestant Churches and Industrial America* (New York: Harper, 1949) 112.
2. Charles Stetzle, "A Son Of the Bowery" in R.C. White Jr. and C.H. Hopkins, *The Social Gospel.*
3. A.B. Simpson, "How Can the Church Reach the Masses," *The Word, Work and World,* Jan. 1882: 24-25.
4. A.B. Simpson, "The Rich and Poor Meet Together," *The Word, Work and World,* Jan. 1882: 25.
5. A.B. Simpson, "The Religious Wants of New York," *The Word, Work and World,* Jan. 1882: 26-28.
6. A.B. Simpson, "Christ and Caste," *The World, Work and World,* Mar. 1882: 122.
7. A.E. Thompson, *A.B. Simpson: His Life and Work,* (Harrisburg: Christian Publications, 1920 revised 1960) 58-61.
8. Thompson 99.
9. Thompson 100-101.
10. G.P. Pardington, *Twenty-five Wonderful Years 1889-1914* (New York: Christian Alliance Publishing Co., 1914) 31.
11. A.E. Funk, "The Homes and Institutions of the Alliance," *The Christian and Missionary Alliance,* 23 Apr. 1897: 393.
12. "The Gospel Tabernacle, New York," *The Word, Work and World,* Mar. 1883: 46.
13. Mrs. Henry Naylor, "Midnight Mission on Twenty-seventh Street," *The Word, Work and World,* June 1883: 93.
14. "Opening of Hephzibah House," *Christian Alliance,* 19 Jan. 1894: 77.
15. "Jerry McAuley's Cremorne Mission," *The Word, Work and World,* June 1883: 92.
16. Charles Gibbord, "The Florence Mission," *The Word,*

Work and World, Nov. 1885: 308.

17. Mrs. Henry Naylor, "First National Convention of Christian Workers," *The Word, Work and World,* Jul. 1886: 31-33.

18. "Work Among the Fallen," *The Word, Work and World,* Feb. 1882: 75.

19. "Reports of Christian Work," *The Word, Work and World,* Oct. 1886: 245.

20. "The Bowery Mission, New York," *The Word, Work and World,* Jan. 1887: 34.

21. "Women's Branch of the City Mission," *The Word, Work and World,* Mar. 1887: 145.

22. "Reports of the Home Work Given at Old Orchard," *Christian Alliance,* 17, Aug. 1895: 161.

23. "Rescue Mission Day at the New York Convention," *Christian Alliance,* 16 Oct. 1895: 253.

24. "Annual Report of the Secretary of the Christian and Missionary Alliance," *Christian Alliance,* 6 Nov. 1895: 300.

25. A.B. Simpson, "The Dark and Bright Side of Christmas," *Christian Alliance,* 25 Dec. 1895: 412.

26. Mrs. A.S. Steele, "Steele Home," *Christian Alliance,* 9 Oct. 1895: 236.

27. A.B. Simpson, editorial, *The Christian and Missionary Alliance,* 7 May 1897: 442.

28. "The City Mission in Williamsport, Pa.," *The Christian and Missionary Alliance,* 26 Mar. 1897: 304.

29. "Our Work in Denver," *The Christian and Missionary Alliance,* 8 June 1898: 544.

30. Henry Wilson, "The Magdalen Home," *The Christian and Missionary Alliance,* 19 Jan. 1898: 64.

31. Mrs. O.S. Schultz, "Berachah Orphanage Work," *Chris-*

tian Alliance, 23 Nov. 1894: 495.

32. Mrs O.S. Schultz, "Berachah Orphanage Work," *Christian Alliance*, 29 May 1895: 348.

33. "Berachah Orphanage," *The Christian and Missionary Alliance*, Apr. 1899: 145.

34. S.H. Hadley, "Rescue Missions," *Christian Alliance*, 25 Sept. 1896: 286.

35. J.G.H. Simpson, "Old Water Street," *The Christian and Missionary Alliance*, 5 Dec. 1903: 12.

36. Miss M. Agnew, "Rescue Mission Work," *The Christian and Missionary Alliance*, 1 June 1901: 305.

37. A.B. Simpson, "Annual Report of the President and General Superintendent of the Christian and Missionary Alliance for the Year 1907-1908," *The Christian and Missionary Alliance*, 6 June 1908: 155.

38. A.B. Simpson, "Our Colored Alliance Brethren," *The Christian and Missionary Alliance*, 9 Mar. 1898: 228.

39. E.B. Nichols, "Work Among Colored People," *The Christian and Missionary Alliance*, 13 July 1898: 41.

40. Mattie A. Bowles, "A Sketch of the Work Being Done in Ohio," *The Christian and Missionary Alliance*, 23 Mar. 1898: 281.

41. A.B. Simpson, "Work Among the Colored People," *The Christian and Missionary Alliance*, 23 Sept. 1899: 265.

42. E.M. Collett, "Our Colored Work," in The Annual Report of The Christian and Missionary Alliance 1910-1911: 79.

43. W.H. Daniels, *Dr. Cullis and His Work* (Boston: Rand, Avery and Co., 1885) 319.

44. "Report of the Committee on Southern Schools, (Colored)," The Annual Report of The Christian and Missionary Alliance 1909-1910: 230.

45. J. Hudson Ballard and R.A. Forrest, "Report of Standing

Committee on Various Schools," The Annual Report of
The Christian and Missionary Alliance 1911-1912: 63.
46. W.S. Rainsford, "Preaching to the Poor," *The Word, Work and World,* Nov. 1885: 312-314.

CHAPTER 6

The Worldwide Social Concern of A.B. Simpson

Surely we may venture as far in undertaking the burdens of Christ's work and the relief of His suffering ones in full assurance that even in the most extreme case, He will prove faithful to us and place at our command His abundant and unfailing resources. What an encouragement to us in the work of His kingdom; in every work before us; in charitable relief for the orphan and the helpless; when done in accordance with His wise and holy will; and in all our spiritual work where we are conscious of our own insufficiency and must constantly venture out in the confidence that He will supply as we go forward, the wisdom, and the power, the faith and the love, the agencies and the efficiency for all our service. (December 23, 1905)

The pages of the magazines edited by A.B. Simpson were filled with reports on world events and how they fit into the total picture of what God was doing in the world. Simpson's interest in world affairs was always seen in the light of the impending return of Jesus Christ. Often biblical prophecies were directly applied to specific countries and events by Simpson. He saw God at work in the political and social world preparing for Christ's return. Hardly a famine or a war went

unnoticed. Natural calamities were also tied by Simpson to
"signs" of the Second Coming. He did not ignore what was
happening but rather publicized the injustices, social ills and
natural calamities occurring around the world. He often
solicited monies and/or goods to help relieve the suffering of
the victims of dislocating events. While rejecting any hope that
social improvement would usher in a millennium of prosperity
and well-being, Simpson called upon his followers to reach out
to aid the unfortunate victims of social ills.

One of the terrible problems in world affairs of the day was
called to the attention of Simpson's readers by a series of
editorials. Of the troubles of Armenians in Turkey Simpson
wrote in 1894, "The most horrible reports have come to us from
central Turkey of unparalleled outrages by the Turks upon the
Armenians, and there is too much reason to fear that these
cruelties have been perpetrated by the connivance of the Turkish
authorities."[1] Simpson deplored the inaction of the European
powers in dealing with this grave situation. He wrote, "The
situation in Turkey is growing every day more critical and
urgent. . . . Each European government is afraid to act separate-
ly, and they are too jealous of each other to be able to act
together."[2] When the European nations were ready to step in
he praised them: "The crisis has become so urgent that all the
great powers of Europe seem at last united in compelling this
crumbling system of impotence and corruption, either to
protect its suffering people or to pass out of the category of
nation."[3] As the atrocities continued Simpson repeatedly spoke
out against them. "The Turkish situation is still very unsettled,"
he wrote. "Massacres almost without intermission, and tens of
thousands of helpless men, women and children, have been
cruelly slain, their homes pillaged, their property destroyed or
stolen, and they, left to face the winter in homelessness, penury

and broken-heartedness." He added, "But there is little reason to hope for the execution of reforms in good faith. The whole system is effete and corrupt."[4] Another editorial continued, "The fearful outrages in Turkey still continue and it is said as many as 60,000 Armenians have suffered outrage and death. Scores and even hundreds of villages have been literally wiped out, . . ."[5]

The Armenian atrocities brought to light Simpson's strong opposition to oppressive governments that would not allow religious freedom and who suppressed minority groups. Each editorial contains reference to God acting to judge and punish Turkey because of its evil deeds. He saw the hand of God moving events toward a final solution, the dissolving of the Turkish government and its tyrannical control over people. The Armenian massacres have been seen by historians as the first modern totalitarian genocide, a foretaste of Hitler and Stalin's holocausts. Simpson made his evangelical readers aware of these events and clearly condemned Turkey as wrong.

Spain's war against Cuba and the subsequent involvement of the United States in a war against Spain was seen, by Simpson, as an act of God to punish an evil nation, Spain. He wrote, "While the spirit of Christianity is pre-eminently for peace, yet God has also a providential purpose in dealing with sinful nations, and sometimes war is one of his scourges."[6]

Even before the United States became involved in the war, *The Christian and Missionary Alliance* carried descriptions of the suffering and starvation in Cuba, with pictures which vividly illustrated the gravity of the situation. This was accompanied by a report by U.S. Senator Proctor detailing conditions inside Cuba.[7] Food and supplies were solicited to be shipped to Cuba under the newly formed Cuban Relief Committee in New York.[8]

When the United States went to war with Spain, Simpson published a justification of the war entitled, "The Significance of the Spanish-American War." He labeled it a "war of humanity" and described it as "a war which no American need ever feel ashamed of," since we were not the aggressor nation. He said that God's will was being fulfilled because Spain was finally being punished for abusing Cuba and for not allowing Protestant missionaries into its colonies.[9] Further explanation of the justness of America's entry into the war was given by Simpson in the editorial "Is War Right?" "We have no doubt whatever that it is a righteous attitude for the American government to interpose for the protection of the outraged Cuban people, just as much as it would be the right of a good Quaker walking down the street and finding a dog devouring a child to attack and save the child." To this argument he added a warning that America put itself above selfishness and seek a speedy conclusion to the war.[10]

Week by week Simpson covered war events: "The President is endeavoring to make war as humane as possible and avoid needless bloodshed."[11] "Spain has been the oppressor of the helpless and has dealt out to the defenseless Cubans the hard measure of famine, disease and death. Now, her people are beginning to taste some of the horrors of famine in the block- aded cities of her own land."[12] "These are the upheavings and mutterings of that great conflict which is ever drawing nearer, and which is to bring at last through earth's final war, the end of war and the golden age of peace and righteousness."[13]

Simpson saw the United States Army as God's agent to open up Cuba and the Philippines to the gospel.[14] "Spain has driven out our missionaries," he noted, "But God has interposed, and a bright dawn has come."[15] He concluded, "We believe that God has planned to break the yoke of political and ecclesiastical bondage by which these millions have so long been held."[16]

When Greece and Turkey were in conflict at the end of the 1890s, Simpson sided with the Greeks. He wrote:

> The Turkish question is the question of prophecy and the question of both hope and fear. Europe has nursed this viper so long that now she knows not what to do with it and God seems to be laughing to scorn the contempt of her powers and suffering them to be wounded for the cruel politic diplomacy that led the helpless maidens and the slaughtered innocents of Armenia to cry in vain for sympathy and help. God, like Himself, has raised up a little one to set at naught their ultimatums and ignoring their diplomacy in the confidence of a just cause practically to defy the world. One cannot but admire the Greeks for their brave and noble stand, and having gone so far it would now be madness for them to retreat. Audacity is their safest course and the European powers may well pause before they let loose their guns on this brave little kingdom, which stands before the public opinion of the world as the champion of freedom and the protector of outraged helplessness.[17]

Looking at conditions in Europe, Asia, Africa and the Americas as the 19th century ended, Simpson concluded, "It is a good time to watch and pray. Above all the clouds the light is shining, and beyond all the over turnings He is coming, coming soon."[18] Each tremble of war, each sign of political upheaval and each prophecy he saw being fulfilled served to heighten his strong belief that the end of the world was approaching. As he wrote, "God is standing back of all these things. . . . It is the purpose of God, and it never was so manifest as it is today, to deal with the nations that have resisted His will."[19]

The situation in the Middle East did not escape Simpson's notice, since it figured so prominently in biblical prophecy. The Jewish reclamation of their "Promised Land" seemed to be an approaching reality at the close of the century. "Never since the destruction of Jerusalem have the political exigencies of the world offered so favorable an opportunity as now for Israel's restoration to Palestine," Simpson asserted in 1894.[20]

Various other world conditions and social and physical needs in the countries of the world were discussed by Simpson and other writers.

The famines in India, during the late 1890s, received substantial coverage, due, in part, to the presence of Alliance missionaries and an orphanage there. A compelling article by Miss E.M. Brickensteen called particular attention to starvation in India:

> In driving along the road one can see poor people sweeping up the dust from the dried-up grass. They winnow what they gather for the sake of the few grass seeds they may find. . . . Children are seen in the streets almost naked, and so weak that they stagger as they walk, glad for a little parched grain that the passerby may give them. A friend writes: "It seems as if I should never get the cry for bread out of my ears."[21]

Another article, "Famine in Central Russia," described the suffering and starvation there.[22] "Opium in Western China" called attention to the ravages of opium and the increase in the number of opium-related suicides there.[23] "The Plague" described the situation in India where rats and disease had caused 86,000 deaths in two years.[24] "The Curse of Africa" pointed out the increase in drunkenness in Africa because of the increased production of gin and rum.[25] "India's Widows" presented the needs of India's poverty-stricken widows.[26] One issue of *The Christian and Missionary Alliance* in 1899 noted a plague in India, a famine in British East Africa and a famine in southern Russia.[27] "The Slave Trade" decried the slave trade among Mohammedans in Africa.[28] "Another Famine in India" was a cover story on the human suffering in India with over three pages of pictures and descriptions.[29] "Vice in Japan" called attention to the growth of prostitution in Japan.[30] "The Famine in India" appealed for aid to be channeled to relieve suffering in India.[31] "Antidotes for Anti-Semitism" urged Christians to correct the prejudice of anti-Jewish feelings.[32] The May, 1899 issue of *The Christian and Missionary Alliance* contained articles on floods in Japan, a famine in northern China, the continuing famine in Russia and plagues in India.[33] "Plague in Alexandria" described the effects of a plague in Egypt.[34] An article on the low social status of women in Chinese society pointed out their deprived lifestyle.[35] Missionary Jennie B. Fuller's book, *Wrongs of Indian Womanhood*, was reviewed in November of 1900.[36]

The above examples illustrate the interest that A.B. Simpson and his followers took in the physical, social and political conditions that impacted the lives of various peoples around the globe. Whether it was the oppression of minority groups, the maltreatment of women in a society, problems with drugs and alcohol or physical disasters like floods and famines, world problems were brought to the attention of Christians in America in order to solicit support in righting wrongs and aiding people. Simpson was interested in more than just the spiritual well-being of humanity, although this was always his primary concern. He also had great sympathy for human suffering, publicized urgent needs and took action to relieve physical problems as well as spiritual ones.

Simpson and his associates responded to human suffering and sought to meet the needs of individuals. Changing the social situation was not their focus. God would ultimately change the situation. In fact, He was already moving among nations to bring about His will. Simpson's response is consistent with what C. Peter Wagner has distinguished as social service.

> *Social service* is the kind of social ministry geared to meet the needs of individuals and groups of persons in a direct and immediate way. If famine comes, social service will provide food for starving people. If an earthquake or tidal wave devastates an area, social service will provide food, clothing, blankets, and medical supplies; also resources to rebuild homes, schools, and churches. If agricultural production is low, social service will introduce new crops, livestock, and farming methods so that food production will increase.[37]

Simpson's approach was not social action. "*Social action* is the kind of social ministry geared toward changing social structures," Wagner notes. "Social action, by definition, involves socio-political changes. . . . The end goal of social action is to substitute just (or more just) for unjust (or less just) political structures."[38] Simpson urged evangelical believers to help alleviate human suffering but he left social transformation entirely in God's more than capable hands. There was a timetable that awaited God's ultimate action.

Endnotes

1. A.B. Simpson, "The Armenian Outrages," *Christian Alliance*, 14 Dec. 1894: 55.

2. A.B. Simpson, "The Turkish Question," *Christian Alliance*, 13 Nov. 1895: 312.

3. A.B. Simpson, "The Eastern Question," *Christian Alliance*, 20 Nov. 1895: 328.

4. A.B. Simpson, "The Outlook in the East," *Christian Alliance*, 18 Dec. 1895: 387.

5. A.B. Simpson, editorial, *Christian Alliance*, 25 Dec. 1895: 412.

6. A.B. Simpson, "War Clouds," *The Christian and Missionary Alliance*, 2 Mar. 1898: 204.

7. A.B. Simpson, "The Situation in the West Indies," *The Christian and Missionary Alliance*, 6 Apr. 1898: 314-315.

8. "Cuban Relief," *The Christian and Missionary Alliance*, 30 Mar. 1898: 301.

9. A.B. Simpson, "The Significance of the Spanish-American War," *The Christian and Missionary Alliance*, 27 Apr. 1898: 396.

10. A.B. Simpson, "Is War Right?" *The Christian and Missionary Alliance*, 4 May 1898: 421.

11. A.B. Simpson, "The Progress of the War," *The Christian and Missionary Alliance*, 4 May 1898: 420.

12. A.B. Simpson, "The Progress of the War," *The Christian and Missionary Alliance*, 11 May 1898: 444.

13. A.B. Simpson, "The Hand of God in Our National Conflict," *The Christian and Missionary Alliance*, 18 May 1898: 468.

14. A.B. Simpson, "The Gospel in Cuba," *The Christian and Missionary Alliance*, 20 July 1898: 76.

15. A.B. Simpson, "Progress," *The Christian and Missionary Alliance*, 15 June 1898: 564.

16. A.B. Simpson, "Prospects," *The Christian and Missionary Alliance*, 3 Aug. 1898: 108.

17. A.B. Simpson, editorial, *The Christian and Missionary Alliance*, 12 Mar. 1897: 252.

18. A.B. Simpson, "The War Cloud Overhanging Europe," *The Christian and Missionary Alliance*, 12 Nov. 1898: 444.

19. A.B. Simpson, "Signs of the Times," *The Christian and Missionary Alliance*, 23 Feb. 1898: 180-181.

20. A.B. Simpson, "Proposed Hebrew Colonization of Palestine," *Christian Alliance*, 27 Apr. 1894: 455.

21. E.M. Brickstein, "A Special Call," *The Christian and Missionary Alliance*, 19 Feb. 1897: 182.

22. "Famine in Central Russia," *Christian Alliance*, 5 Nov. 1895: 426.

23. "Opium in Western China," *The Christian and Missionary Alliance*, 26 Oct. 1898: 402.

24. "The Plague," *The Christian and Missionary Alliance*, 5 Nov. 1898: 426.

25. "The Curse of Africa," *The Christian and Missionary Alliance*, 7 Oct. 1899: 368.

26. "India's Widows," *The Christian and Missionary Alliance*, 5 Aug. 1899: 158.

27. "Field Notes," *The Christian and Missionary Alliance*, 19 Aug. 1899: 190.

28. "The Slave Trade," *The Christian and Missionary Alliance*, 14 Oct. 1899: 322.

29. "Another Famine in India," *The Christian and Missionary Alliance*, 25 Nov. 1899: 405-407+.

30. "Vice in Japan," *The Christian and Missionary Alliance*, 25 Nov. 1899: 418.

31. "The Famine in India," *The Christian and Missionary Alliance*, 2 Dec. 1899: 429.

32. F.W. Farr, "Antidotes for Anti-Semitism," *The Christian and Missionary Alliance*, Jan. 1898: 40.

33. "Field Notes," *The Christian and Missionary Alliance*, May 1899: 190.

34. "Plague in Alexandria," *The Christian and Missionary Alliance*, 2 Dec. 1899: 435.

35. Mary E. Parmenter, "The Condition of Women in China," *The Christian and Missionary Alliance*, 23 Dec. 1899: 470-471.

36. *Wrongs of Indian Womanhood*, by Jennie B. Fuller, book review, *The Christian and Missionary Alliance*, 10 Nov. 1900.

37. C. Peter Wagner, "A Missiological View of Christian Relief and Development," *Christian Relief and Development: Developing Workers for Effective Ministry*, ed. Edgar J. Elliston (Dallas: Word Publishing, 1989) 122.

38. Wagner 122.

CHAPTER 7

The Social Message of the Theology of A.B. Simpson

[The Cross of Christ] regenerates the human heart. It puts a new nature in man, it makes the sinner automatically right, not driven by force or fear to keep some inexorable law, but drawn by the constraint of his own desire to do what God would have him to do and be what God would have him be. It puts a self-acting principle in every saved man, which produces the fruit of righteousness just as naturally as a vine produces grapes and a rose produces fragrance.

. . . it creates practical righteousness between man and man. It substitutes the golden rule for the maxims of human policy, and teaches men to "deny ungodliness and worldly lusts, and to live soberly, righteously and godly in this present evil world," and leads men to desire a religion that can change a pick-pocket into an honest man and a cursing virago into a gentle saint.

. . . it elevates human society, gives freedom to the slave, sets women free from degradation and shame, builds every hospital that ever sheltered a sufferer, sends its red cross banner to the battle field, and better still, teaches the nations to turn their swords into plow-shares and study war no more. (August 3, 1907)

A.B. Simpson formulated much of his theology and conducted much of his ministry against the backdrop of the optimistic humanism of liberal theology, yet his theology was a reaffirmation of the older, conservative, evangelical tradition. Facing the same social forces of upheaval and the demands of progress and change as liberal theologians faced, he called for a return to the theological doctrines of personal salvation and hope in the visible, triumphant return of Jesus Christ. The second coming of Christ played a key role in his theology as well as his view of world conditions. He believed that efforts to evangelize the world would actually hasten the Lord's return. Simpson saw the world of his day through eyes that were focused on the returning Christ. Social transformation would transpire only when Christ returned to establish His millennial kingdom.

The Failure of Humanism

The failure of human wisdom to cope with social and spiritual problems is a recurrent theme in Simpson's writings. His book *Is Life Worth Living?* strongly criticized human efforts to reform society and human wisdom to meet spiritual needs. He wrote, "Science has built its temples in each successive generation only to find them dissolve before the keen gaze of the next generation. Philosophy has launched into the realm of speculation only to find how little its cold conclusions and ideal speculations could satisfy the human soul and take the place of man's immortal mind."[1]

The greatest of human effort to better society will fail, Simpson believed, therefore, philanthropic efforts necessarily took a decidedly secondary position in his theology and ministry. As he put it:

We may turn from pursuits of commerce, from the

dream of pleasure, and devote ourselves to the work of human philanthropy, to temperance and social reform, to good government clubs and political conflicts against the evils of society, and all these have their places, but, alas, they are under the sun, and they shall end like Solomon's dream in vanity and vexation. We shall clean the Augean stables of politics today to find them filthier than ever tomorrow with a new herd of time servers and selfish boodlers, and we shall find out perhaps too late that the only remedy for earth's wrongs is the coming of the Lord Jesus Christ and the kingdom of His grace and glory. Let the world do its best, but why should we devote the strength of our lives to the second best when we have God's best remedy for the wrongs of earth and the ills of time?[2]

Simpson detected a fatal flaw in the human character which ultimately made all efforts at human betterment and perfection doomed to failure from the start. He gave the following illustration to demonstrate that flaw:

It is said that a costly building once fell in ruins and the committee were engaged amid the wreck in trying to explain the cause. The architect produced his plans, and they were perfect. The arches were all right, and the supporting pillars and buttresses were in their places. But just then a common worker passing by picked up a brick from among the ruins, and crumbled it to dust between his fingers, laughed and said: "All the plans in the world could not make that building safe. The material is worthless. The brick is unburned, and crumbles at a touch into a heap of sand."

This is the answer to all your theories of social reform, the material is useless. The brick is unburned. The essential elements of human nature are wrong and hopeless. Man needs more than reformation; he needs a new creation and a divine nature.[3]

Surveying the entire international scene, Simpson came to the conclusion that, "the best of human governments have failed." He saw only one clear solution, "There is but one Hope, but one King, and He will soon step upon the troubled scene, and set up His peaceful throne."[4]

Simpson commented on the disastrous results of humanism in *The Gospel of the Kingdom*. He painted a full picture of the condition of mankind under the godless humanism he saw growing in intensity all around him:

Our golden age is far from unfolding even the promise of a Millennium. Beyond any past age, science, invention, intelligence and education have reached a lofty level, but human wisdom is a Greek arch, rising above the earth only to curve back to earth again, instead of a Gothic arch, whose highest reach points still upward. The material conditions of the world may advance only to develop materialism, magnifying things seen and temporal, obscuring the unseen and eternal. What is the real character of our present civilization? We may as well face the facts. It is gigantic in invention, discovery, enterprise, achievement, but it is gigantically worldly— sometimes and somewheres monstrously God-denying and God-defying. This "Christian civilization" has produced giants in these days, men of renown, but they often use their intellect, knowledge and fame only to break down, as with iron flail of Talus, the Christian faith. Philosophy now blooms into a refined and poetic pantheism or a gross, blind materialism, or a subtle rationalism, or an absurd agnosticism. Science constructs its system of evolution and leaves out a personal God; spontaneous generation becomes the only creator, natural law the only determining power, and natural selection the only providence. Such men as Strauss and Renan, Hegel and Comte, Goethe and Kant, Mills and Spencer, Darwin and Huxley, Matthew Arnold and Theodore Parker, are specimens of men who owe their education, refinement, accomplishment to the very Christianity they attack. The cubs first nurse the dam and then turn and strike their fangs into her breast. Civilization itself is turned into the stronghold of unbelief: its imaginations and inventions are hightowers that exalt themselves against the knowledge of God, and the thoughts of our great thinkers have not been brought into captivity to the obedience of Christ.

We have the ripest form of worldly civilization, but the ripeness borders on rottenness; while men boast of the fabric its foundations are falling into decay, and that awful anarchy which is the last of atheism even now threatens to dissolve society itself.[5]

While liberal theologians were predicting the arrival of a golden age of progress and a "kingdom of God" here on earth, Simpson searched for evidence to support this supposed new era for humanity. He did not have to look far to see just the opposite. In 1898 he wrote, "We need look no further than our own country to see how far off is any spiritual millennium even from the most advanced of Christian countries."[6]

The Mission of the Church

The mission of the church, for Simpson, was not to reform society but to rescue a few souls from the sinking ship of humanity. Personal salvation, rather than social salvation, was to be the message of Simpson and the Alliance.

Simpson delivered a message at Old Orchard Beach, Maine in 1907 which noted that man's philanthropic aims to improve this world were not what God had in mind. He proclaimed, "No, God's wisdom and love have something better for our race than civilization, reformation, social reform and scientific progress; something better even than a spiritual millennium and the worldwide triumph of the Gospel of the grace of God." Rather, he said, "Just as for the individual God's highest thought is not self-improvement, nor reformation, not the best possible result out of our natural character and human culture, but a new creation, a regeneration so complete that old things pass away and all things are made new; so for the world itself God's plan is the same." He added, "The City of God does not spring up from the earth, but as the new Jerusalem, it comes down from heaven."[7]

Premillennialism

The second coming of Christ is going to be premillennial, according to Simpson. No earthly kingdom of brotherhood, love and progress is going to precede the visible, physical return of Christ for his saints.

"The Pre-Millennial Coming of the Lord," an 1894 article in *The Christian Alliance*, discussed the millennium and when it will commence. Simpson raised scriptural objections to the notion of a millennial kingdom of God on earth prior to the return of Christ. He wrote, "Our Lord tells us that when He comes again, the world will not be in a condition of truth and righteousness, but rather in a state of godlessness and worldliness." He pointed out the biblical picture of the last days as being like Noah's times, with evil and godlessness running unchecked. He viewed the world as getting steadily worse, instead of better. He concluded, "There will be no millennium before the Lord's return. . . . Our Lord never allowed us to assume that there was to be a fixed period of a thousand years of spiritual blessing, or of anything else before His personal return."[8]

Early in his independent ministry, Simpson traced a shift in his beliefs about the second coming of Christ. He wrote, "I was trained in the Scottish school of theology, and was taught to consider Christ's coming to mean His manifestation to the soul of the believer by the Spirit, His coming at death to the saint, and His coming spiritually by the spread of the Gospel." He said that he continued to believe this way until his revival experience under the ministry of Major Whittle in Louisville. At that time, he wrote, "I saw that the idea of the growth of a spiritual millennium was unscriptural; the world was becoming worse and worse." He came to realize that the end times would be marked by what he described as a "great falling away, and new and dreadful forms of evil."[9]

Ernest Sandeen's description of premillennialists, in *The Roots of Fundamentalism*, fits Simpson quite well:

> Converts to premillennialism abandoned confidence in man's ability to bring about significant and lasting social progress and in the church's ability to stem the tide of evil, convert mankind to Christianity, or even prevent its own corruption. The premillennial return of Christ presupposed a view of the world in which judgment and

demolition were the only possible response from a just
God. Christ's return would mean salvation for a few but
judgment for the world.[10]

Tracing premillennialism in America to British sources, Sandeen finds the seed-bed of the movement in this country in Bible
and prophecy conferences held in the last half of the nineteenth
century. He mentions A.J. Gordon, A.T. Pierson, D.L. Moody
and F.B. Meyer as men who either participated in these conferences or held premillennial views.[11] These men shared
Simpson's New York pulpit and Simpson spoke in their churches during that era, although Simpson did not totally agree
with them on eschatological matters, particularly dispensationalism. Sandeen also mentions D.W. Whittle, Simpson's
evangelist while in Louisville, as a familiar leader of some of
these conferences.[12] It is safe to assume that Simpson had been
theologically influenced by Whittle and these others even
though he never directly participated in the prophetic conferences that gave birth to dispensational premillennialism.

In *The Coming One*, written in 1912, Simpson remarked that
one only had to look at the headlines of any daily newspaper to
see that things were getting worse and not better.[13] Similar
sentiments were expressed repeatedly in his sermons and writings.

"The Quest of Wisdom," a sermon preached by Simpson at
the Missionary Training Institute in Nyack, New York, on May
23, 1909, once again called attention to the failure of human
effort to rectify conditions in an increasingly evil world. He told
the students, "The dark blot of poverty, sickness and vice has
proved too well that humanity has failed to meet the real
problems of life." He continued, "The radical and fatal trouble
with humanity is that it is wrong with God and wrong at heart.

It has departed from its divine center and has wandered into darkness, sin, sorrow, death and eternal despair. And before it can ever be made happy it must be made right." He told them that it all came down to the question, "How shall we make bad men good?" He rejected punishment as destructive, good examples as powerless and legalism as reaching only the head and not the heart. He proposed the saving gospel of Jesus Christ, which makes individuals new creations, thereby modifying their behavior toward their fellow men, as the only hope for remedying man's condition.[14]

Simpson's social theory, as we noted above, has been categorized as *symptomatic* or *relief-oriented premillennialism by* Douglas Matthews.[15] Suffering individuals were ministered to but the social structure that produced the suffering was left in God's hands.

The Failure of the Modern Church

Not only had humanism and philanthropy failed to make the world better, Simpson charged, but the church had also failed in its mission. It had become embroiled in theological disputes, and, worst of all, it had compromised itself with the world. By abandoning the message of personal salvation, wrote Simpson, "She sat down in the little circle of her own religious selfishness, and left a thousand million of her family to perish without truth."[16]

In "The Perils of the Modern Church," written in 1897, Simpson equated the church of his day with the church of Laodicea, mentioned in the book of Revelation. He wrote:

> Laodicea represents the closing chapter of church history, and the picture of our own times. It is a church with Jesus Christ outside knocking for admission to His

own temple. It is the church perfectly satisfied with itself, and boasting of its riches and its spiritual condition, telling of the number of its adherents, and pointing to the magnificence of its sanctuaries and organization. But, alas, when you feel its pulse! The Master turns away with loathing and disgust; it is the lukewarm, it is the spiritually indifferent, it is given over to self-complacency, luxury and respectability.[17]

He castigated the average American church for its worldly materialism, in "The Curse of Selfishness," in 1904. He described the typical lifestyle of the average church member as life all wrapped up in clothes, houses, furnishings, decorations, parties, vacations and material excesses.[18]

The hidden corruption in nominal Christians was presented as "leaven" in the church by Simpson, in a sermon in 1903 entitled "The Parables of the Kingdom." He said that leaven represented evil, rather than good, as some had interpreted it. "It represents unbelief, the worldliness, the selfishness, the license which today are slowly wearing down the barriers of faith, conscience and separation even in the church itself, and reducing society to one broad level of liberalism, humanitarianism and easy going selfishness."[19]

Simpson labeled the church's failure to remain true to its divine mission "Christianity's crime." He compared the uncaring church of his day to a man who told people that he was setting up an orphanage for poor children and solicited funds but then spent the monies on himself instead. The church was to be rescuing men from sin but was living in selfishness and luxury instead.[20] Simpson wrote in 1895, "Never will the world be saved by compromise with it, but only by standing on God's level, and lifting men up to our side."[21]

The modern church had lost the blessing of God's Spirit working in it, Simpson maintained, due to its worldliness, materialism, lack of belief and compromise with human philosophy. He noted in 1897 that, "There is an evident withdrawal of the convicting and converting power of the Holy Spirit from the ordinary channels of Christian work." He labeled most modern revivals "man-made," and charged that the church had brought worldly entertainments in to replace the preaching of the gospel. However, he pointed out, "In the humble rescue mission and among the neglected classes of the slums and the highways and hedges, the Gospel is still working with its ancient power, but this is a movement from the centre, a movement downward to the lower strata of human life."[22] He saw a church within a church in his day: "Everywhere throughout Christendom it is the same," he noted, "a little church within a larger church, a little flock of hungry, holy ones, walking with the Saviour . . . in the midst of a great mass of worldly-minded, pleasure loving Christians, who have a form of godliness but practically deny the power thereof."[23]

The idea of a "holy" church within a larger worldly church shows the influence of the Holiness movement on Simpson. With the Holiness movement Simpson shared an emphasis on the deeper life which called the believer on to a higher, more intense level of commitment. The result was a church within a church. Those who professed Christ and were believers and those who, likewise, professed belief in Christ and went on to a fuller dedication to holy living and Christian service. Vinson Synan, in *The Holiness-Pentecostal Movement in the United States*, names Simpson and the Alliance as sharing the theology of the Holiness movement, even though the Alliance "had their beginnings in the period before the doctrine of sanctification became controversial."[24] According to Synan, "During the

1880's the holiness awakening reached its peak of acceptance and popularity in America."[25] The Christian and Missionary Alliance came into existence during the 1880s under Simpson's guidance. The influence of the holiness movement on Simpson and the movement which he founded were profound.

Tracing the roots of the Holiness movement back to early Methodism and the Wesleys, Synan points out elements of Methodism which Simpson shared wholeheartedly. "If the Calvinist taught that only the elect could be saved, the Methodist taught that anyone could find salvation," wrote Synan. "If the Calvinist could never be certain that he was in the elect circle, the Methodist could know from a crisis experience of conversion that he was saved."[26] Simpson emphasized the openness of salvation to all, as well as a crisis experience of salvation and sanctification, similar to that which he himself had experienced under Whittle earlier in his ministry.

The Relation to the Second Coming

Convinced that he was living in the last days, Simpson repeatedly sought to find some verification of this in the Bible. In the process of proving the reality of the nearness of Christ's return, he shared some of the views of dispensationalism. He saw history as made up of ages, patterned after stages derived from the book of Revelation's description of the Seven Churches of Asia. While Simpson was clearly influenced by dispensationalists, it would be incorrect to label him a dispensationalist. The sermon "The Christian Age," published in 1912, lays out his views on the matter. It was a sermon delivered to throw light on "the utter unscripturalness of post-millennial theory, or the prospect of a millennium without Christ."[27] Simpson defined the real church as, "an invisible society, consisting of all who are born again." The visible church was defined as "the representative of the Lord on earth and His witness to the world, and notwithstanding its imperfections it enjoys the presence of the Master."[28] He was convinced that the visible church would not become purer through history but, rather, increasingly apostate. He warned, "The Church of Apostles became the apostasy of Rome and the Church of the Reformation appears in even greater danger of developing into the Laodicea of the Apocalypse, if not the Babylon of God's last and most terrible judgment."[29]

Simpson discussed the seven parables of Matthew chapter thirteen, which he applied to the condition of the church in various ages; the parable of the tares represented the planting of errors and heresies in the early church; the parable of the mustard seed showed that the church would grow into a worldly institution with birds, representing evil, living in its branches; the leaven parable foreshadowed the great apostasy of the 6th and 7th centuries; the parable of the pearl showed a treasure, the true church, hidden within the false; and the parable of the drawing of the nets revealed the final separation between true and false church members.

Turning to the book of Revelation, Simpson asserted, "Once more in the Seven Epistles to the churches of Asia, our Lord's last word to the present age, we have what appears to the most thoughtful expositors an historical panorama of the successive stages of visible Christianity from the vision of Patmos to the end of time."[30] He coupled these epistles to the church in different stages of its history. "The church in Ephesus, orthodox, active, conservative and growing cold, represents the second generation of primitive Christians;" Smyrna, the suffering church persecuted by Rome; Pergamos, the church of Constantine exalted to power and wealth, yet corrupted by the world; Thyatira, "a true and vivid picture of the rise of

Romanism and all its deep and devilish wiles and widespread
domination over the church of God from the sixth to the
sixteenth century;" Sardis, "the putrid corpse of Medieval
Romanism;" Philadelphia, the church of the Reformation; and
Laodicea, modern Protestantism, the "church of wealth and
pride, but so languid and lukewarm that the impatient Master
is about to reject it as a nauseous offense." He concluded by
claiming that "there is a holy Philadelphia even amid an insipid
Laodicea. May He find us with the little flock to whom it is the
Father's good pleasure to give the kingdom!"[31]

In 1887 Simpson warned, "The Church of Christ is getting
farther from the masses of our population and more deeply into
worldliness, unbelief and barrenness."[32] He believed that the
purpose of his independent ministry was to evangelize those the
church-at-large had forgotten, the poor and neglected at home
and abroad. He reemphasized this in 1899 in "The Mission of
the Alliance," where he wrote,

> Let us never forget the special calling of our Alliance
> work. It is not to form a new religious denomination.
> It is not to duplicate a work already done. It is not to
> advocate any special system of theology. It is not to
> glorify any man or men. It is first to hold up Jesus in
> His fulness, "the same yesterday, today and forever."
> Next, to lead God's hungry children to know their full
> inheritance of privilege and blessing for spirit, soul and
> body. Next, to witness to the imminent coming of the
> Lord Jesus Christ as our millennial King. And finally,
> to encourage and incite the people of God to do the
> neglected work of our age and time among the unchur-
> ched classes at home and the perishing heathen
> abroad.[33]

In his annual report on the work of The Christian and Missionary Alliance for the 1908-1909 year, Simpson could claim, "we know of no work which represents so large a gathering out, not only from the world, but from the worldly church, OUT AND OUT, of so many simple hearted, self-sacrificing and wholly consecrated followers of the meek and lowly Jesus."[34]

The Missionary Enterprise and the Second Coming

Simpson preached from Luke chapter fourteen on several occasions. Two published sermons on this text, both titled "Aggressive Christianity," give insight into the biblical basis of Simpson's desire to take the gospel to the neglected peoples of the world.

The parable of the feast was used to illustrate God's effort to call to himself three classes of people. The first were those who received a double invitation and, yet, rejected both calls. "They represent in our day," he said, "the ordinary hearers of the Gospel, the children of the Kingdom, the people who have inherited the privileges of Christianity as a kind of birthright."[35] He labeled them "The Satisfied"; they were the rich and happy church-goers who were wrapped up in the materialism of the day.[36]

When the well-off spurned their invitation, a messenger was sent out into the streets to invite others in. These he labeled "The Suffering"; they were the poor, the sorrowing, those whom Christ came to save.[37] Simpson called this "a movement downward. It is the gospel for the slums, it is the gospel mission work. It is the love that is going from the fashionable circles and ordinary walks to gather pearls amid the lost masses of our great city."[38]

The third class invited into the feast were the lepers and

outcasts, representing the heathen. The invitation was to go out to "the outcasts of humanity that lie beyond the vale of Christianity."[39] They were seemingly beyond all hope, beyond all morality or religion, yet, the Savior cared especially for them.[40] Simpson believed that the gospel being proclaimed with the most success in his day was the "gospel of practical religion," which was being of real help for human suffering and the "gospel of healing," which with compassion was reaching the poor and diseased.[41]

Simpson tied the second coming of Christ to world evangelization. "The work of missions is the great means of hastening the end," he wrote in *The Coming One*. "Until the whole number of His elect shall have thus been called and gathered home, His second coming would seem to be delayed."[42] The same connection was made in *The Gospel of the Kingdom*, where he wrote, "One of the most definite of all the signs given by our Lord is this: 'This Gospel of the Kingdom must first be published in all the world as a witness unto all nations, and then shall the end come.' This gives to the work of missions a peculiar interest and responsibility."[43] Simpson believed that this missionary obligation was rapidly being accomplished in his day. Missions was the project to which he devoted most of his energy.

The Kingdom of God

Simpson believed that the mission of the church was to evangelize the world, to rescue a few men from the doomed world. This view of the mission of the church was at odds with the main thrust of American Protestantism at the close of the nineteenth and start of the twentieth century. The book that spells out his disagreement with the "new theology" of his day is *The Old Faith and the New Gospels*, which appeared in 1911.

Simpson argued against the "Post-Millennialists" of the day.

"The great mass of Modern Protestants are expecting no other millennium and no higher manifestation of the kingdom of God on earth than that which is to come about through civilization, the spread of the Gospel and the progress of Christianity among the nations,"[44] he wrote. He disagreed with those who "try to cultivate character" apart from the work of Christ on the cross. He saw such a viewpoint as worthless, powerless and ineffective.[45] In response to the claim of social gospel theologians that all one needs to do is to imitate the life of Jesus and practice the social principles of Jesus, Simpson wrote, "But we need more than teaching, ideals and examples. We need motive power. . . . I need Jesus of Nazareth Himself within me to walk in His footsteps."[46]

In *The Old Faith and the New Gospels* Simpson defined true Christianity, and by so doing he refuted the "new gospels" of his day. He stated,

> Therefore Christianity begins with a new creation, a new nature, a new heart, a divine root and principle of righteousness, goodness, virtue and holiness. Christ does not ask unregenerate men to be good. "That which is born of the flesh is flesh." "The carnal mind is enmity against God for it is not subject to the mind of God, neither indeed can it be. So then they that are in the flesh cannot please God." The Gospel simply asks the sinner to stop all his doing, to give up his dead works and to receive Jesus Christ and through Him that divine life that will in its own inherent nature lead him to love the good, to hate the evil and to follow righteousness by a "law of the fitness of things." This is the Gospel. And all the humanism of our day and the codes of our day fail because in the pride of human self-righteousness

they "are going about to establish their own righteousness and have not submitted themselves to the
righteousness of God."[47]

The true, biblical picture of the coming of the kingdom of
God, Simpson believed, would be a supernatural event. "It is
the kingdom which is to come with the coming of the King,"
he wrote. "It is to be inaugurated by the personal return of the
Lord Jesus Christ Himself and to be consummated by His
personal reign throughout the millennial age." Simpson stated
clearly, "It is not an evolution from the forces of human
civilization but a revolution bursting upon an astonished world,
not blending with men's selfish and imperfect achievements,
but superseding all earthly sovereignties with His own supreme
and everlasting dominion."[48]
What will be the nature of this kingdom according to
Simpson? "It is to be a kingdom of righteousness, peace on earth
and good will to men," he wrote. "The victims of oppression
will weep no more. Poverty, injustice and wrong will be but
memories of the departed day. Sickness will be unknown, death
itself will at last be dead." To this image he added, "Every earthly
relationship will be perfectly harmonized. Every person will find
his true place. Every capacity and power will be utilized for the
happiness of each and the benefit of the whole."[49]
This was the message of A.B. Simpson and the movement
known as The Christian and Missionary Alliance. Converted
individuals would make society better, rather than a converted
society making individuals better. Instead of a gradual progress
toward a better or more Christian person, Simpson taught a
gospel of instantaneous conversion, which did not mean sinless
perfection, but power from the indwelling Christ to live for
good and oppose evil.[50]

Writing on the purpose and responsibility of The Christian and Missionary Alliance, Simpson declared,

> Instead of all this humanitarian philosophy the Alliance movement stands for the old faith and hope of the primitive church, the coming of the Lord Jesus Christ, the establishment of a kingdom that is not of this world and the bringing down of the "new Jerusalem from God out of heaven," not as an evolution of human society, but as a revolution of divine power and victory. We are not building a temple on earth, but sending on the materials to the great Architect who is to bring it with Him from the skies. This gives character and aim to all our work. The inspiration of our personal lives and our missionary and evangelistic endeavors is not to create an organization here that will be perfect or permanent, but to prepare the way of the Lord and hasten His personal return. The one solution we offer for every earthly problem, the one remedy we propose for every human wrong is the coming of our Lord and the establishment upon earth of His everlasting kingdom of peace and righteousness. [51]

In "Christ's Coming the Key to All Questions of the Age," Simpson summarized his views on the coming kingdom.

> The personal and premillennial coming of our Lord is the true key to history, to the social and political problems of the age, and to the work of the church. . . . This is the true remedy for the social ills of our time. The wise Christian will give his strength today not to reform or mere philanthropy, but to hastening the

coming of the King, which alone will right earth's wrongs and redress her grievances. And this is the only standpoint from which the church can do her work effectively. If she is setting out to convert the world and battle its gigantic evils we may well give up the conflict in despair, but if she understands her mission to gather out of the nations a people for His name she will have abundant cause for encouragement, and she will know that her work is not in vain in the Lord, as one by one she is calling out members of the Bride to meet the coming Lord and sending wedding cards to all the world for the marriage of the Lamb. This is our vocation.[52]

Endnotes

1. A.B. Simpson, *Is Life Worth Living?* (South Nyack, NY: Christian Alliance Publishing Co., 1899) 14-15.
2. Simpson, *Life* 46-47.
3. Simpson, *Life* 23-24.
4. A.B. Simpson, *The Gospel of the Kingdom* (New York: Christian Alliance Publishing Co., 1890) 191-192.
5. Simpson, *Kingdom* 205-206.
6. A.B. Simpson, "Missions and Premillennialism," *The Christian and Missionary Alliance*, 26 Oct. 1898: 396.
7. A.B. Simpson, "The Lord's Coming and Missions," *The Christian and Missionary Alliance*, 31 Aug. 1907: 98.
8. A.B. Simpson, "The Pre-Millennial Coming of the Lord," *Christian Alliance*, 10 Aug. 1894: 130.
9. A.B. Simpson, "The Second Coming of Christ," *The Word, Work and World*, Nov. 1885: 315-316.
10. Ernest Sandeen, *The Roots of Fundamentalism* (Chicago: Univ. of Chicago Press, 1970) 13-14.

11. Sandeen 142-143.
12. Sandeen 174.
13. A.B. Simpson, *The Coming One* (New York: Christian Alliance Publishing Co., 1912) 188.
14. A.B. Simpson, "The Quest of Wisdom," *The Christian and Missionary Alliance*, 5 June 1909: 164.
15. Douglas K. Matthews. "Approximating the Millennium: Toward a Coherent Premillennial Theology of Social Transformation," diss., Baylor University, 1992: 63-64.
16. A.B. Simpson, "The Significance of Our Times," *Christian Alliance*, 19 Oct. 1894: 372.
17. A.B. Simpson, "The Perils of the Modern Church," *The Christian and Missionary Alliance*, 8 Jan. 1897: 34-35.
18. A.B. Simpson, "The Curse of Selfishness," *The Christian and Missionary Alliance*, 17 Sept. 1904: 254.
19. A.B. Simpson, "The Parables of the Kingdom," *The Christian and Missionary Alliance*, 26 Dec. 1903: 45.
20. A.B. Simpson, *Missionary Messages* (New York: Christian Alliance Publishing Co., 1925) 76-77.
21. A.B. Simpson, "Separation," *Christian Alliance*, 11 Sept. 1895: 170.
22. A.B. Simpson, untitled editorial, *The Christian and Missionary Alliance*, 15 Jan. 1897: 60.
23. A.B. Simpson, "A Church Within a Church," *Christian Alliance*, 29 May 1895: 344.
24. Vinson Synan, *The Holiness-Pentecostal Movement in the United States* (Grand Rapids: Eerdman's, 1971) 59-60.
25. Synan 43.
26. Synan 14.
27. A.B. Simpson, "The Christian Age, *The Alliance Weekly*, 10 Feb. 1912: 291.
28. Simpson, "Age" 291.

29. Simpson, "Age" 292.

30. Simpson, "Age" 292.

31. Simpson, "Age" 292-293.

32. A.B. Simpson, "Distinctive Teachings," *The Word, Work and World,* July 1887: 3.

33. A.B. Simpson, "The Mission of the Alliance," *The Christian and Missionary Alliance,* 4 Nov. 1899: 365.

34. A.B. Simpson, "President's Report of the Work," *The Christian and Missionary Alliance,* 5 June 1909: 153.

35. A.B. Simpson, "Aggressive Christianity," *Christian Alliance,* 27 Nov. 1895: 345.

36. A.B. Simpson, "Aggressive Christianity," *The Christian and Missionary Alliance,* 15 Sept. 1900: 148.

37. Simpson, "Aggressive" 1900: 148

38. Simpson, "Aggressive," 1895: 345.

39. Simpson, "Aggressive" 1895: 345.

40. Simpson, "Aggressive," 1900: 149.

41. Simpson, "Aggressive," 1895: 345.

42. Simpson, *Coming* 220, 222.

43. Simpson, *Kingdom* 215.

44. Simpson, *Old* 133.

45. Simpson, *Old* 89-90.

46. Simpson, *Old* 90-91.

47. Simpson, *Old* 91.

48. Simpson, *Old* 136.

49. Simpson, *Old* 138, 140.

50. A.B. Simpson, "Our Trust," *The Christian and Missionary Alliance,* 28 May 1910: 145.

51. Simpson, "Our Trust" 146.

52. A.B. Simpson, "Christ's Coming the Key to All Questions of the Age," *The Christian and Missionary Alliance,* 9 Mar. 1898: 228-229.

CHAPTER 8

The Social Responsibilities of Christians

There is a place for social differences and they exist in the nature of things. God does not come with an iconoclastic hand to sweep away all differences and bring a hopeless socialism. There are differences. They grow out of successful lives, they can be maintained with sweetness and the door can be left open for ambition to rise to the highest possibilities. But let there be no harshness. Let the doors be wide open and the spirit of love and sympathy meet from both sides. God recognizes this and bids us "render . . . to all their dues." Impudence and insolence is not part of the gospel of Jesus Christ. Courtesy and respect to all classes and in all places is one of the qualities of true Christian humility. But this is very different from exclusiveness and pride. The true church should be a mission too. So in our family, social and business lives let us carry out this law of love with proper respect and honor for all, and yet loving consideration, a spirit of considerateness for those in humbler places, the graciousness that in every way covers our social differences by Christ's own law of love. (1901)

The fact that A.B. Simpson, his colleagues and those he influenced conducted social work in the form of rescue missions, orphanages and other benevolent ministries, both in North America and overseas, has been established above. The theology of A.B. Simpson has been contrasted to the Social Gospel theology of his era. Reference has been made to his published reports on social and physical problems around the world. We now turn to look at some of the practical remarks he made about how Christians should relate to wealth, possessions, the needs of less fortunate people and how Christians can aid the disadvantaged.

Material Luxury Versus Christian Service

Simpson often attacked the way of life of those in his day who lived only for material things and who forgot the eternal and spiritual matters. In a sermon preached in 1905 entitled "The Right and Wrong Way of Living," he grieved for the multitudes who were spending their lives in the pursuit of outward, material possessions. He said, "How often we see money spent lavishly in accumulating the mere materials of life; houses, land, equipage, income and the whole machinery of life, but when it is accomplished, it is hollow at heart."[1] Wealth and possessions, even education and culture, would be empty if they were not put to use for God.

He called the Christian's attention to the fact that their faith was a trust given to them to be a benefit to mankind and that all they had was a gift from God. He asked,

What must the Heavenly Father think as His poor perishing children are lifting up their wan faces and their bony fingers in entreaty to Him, and going forth in one long and ceaseless procession of despair to their eternal destiny while we are enjoying the hopes and privileges which cost our Redeemer His precious life, and saying with self-complacency, "I am rich and increased with goods and have need of nothing." Surely the day will come when His voice of thunder will shake us from our indifference as it calls in our ears, "The voice of thy brother's blood crieth unto Me from the ground! Where is the soul of thy brother?"[2]

What Christians did with their money, their goods and with the spiritual trust of salvation given to them, Simpson felt, would determine their judgment before a righteous God.

The servanthood of Christ was seen by Simpson as the believer's example. The Christian was called to serve. He declared, "He Himself made Himself the servant of all, and he who would come nearest to Him and stand closest to Him at the last, must likewise learn the spirit of the ministry that has utterly renounced selfish rights and claims forever."[3]

Christians were called to be representatives of Christ in the world. In a sermon in 1894, Simpson told the congregation, "We are not sent here to make a living, or to make money . . . our one business is to represent Him here. . . . While engaged in the secular affairs of life, it is simply that we may represent Him there, carry on His business and have means to use for His affairs."[4]

Simpson came down harshly on the waste and extravagance in which some Christians were living. In "God's Compensation" he wrote,

> The surplus and waste which professing Christians are expending in absolute needless indulgence, in extra buttons on their gloves, extra furniture in their homes, extra splendor in their equipage, extra houses for their residence in town and country, extra decorations on

their churches, extra music in their choirs, these useless,
wasteful things alone would be sufficient, if given to
God, to evangelize the entire world in a decade of years.[5]

He was very concerned that God's work be done and had little
patience with those who wanted nothing more out of their lives
or religion than to sit back in selfish comfort while the world
remained in need.

On a very practical level, he urged Christians to receive the
poor and needy into their churches with warm, open arms of
acceptance. "We are not to try to get up an elite company of
congenial, pleasant Christian associates, in every way desirable,"
Simpson preached, "but we are to accept all the conditions
which God has mingled in this world, and to receive them in
His name. . . . The most profitable church in which one's lot
can be cast, and the very best school in which our character can
be developed, is just a combination of various elements, and
even trying surroundings."[6]

Sanctification Not Social Isolation

Sanctification, for Simpson, did not mean isolation from the
needs of a dying world. "I should greatly suspect my sanctification if it led me to lose my interest in the salvation of men, and
my love for the souls of the lost and unworthy," he wrote.
"Thank God that in these days the men and women that are
going the deepest into the slums and searching the farthest for
the sheep that have gone astray, are those who believe in the
fulness of Christ."[7] Rather than going inward into selfish Christian living, Simpson saw the fruits of sanctification to be a
greater concern for the needs of others. Instead of isolation in
comfortable Christian conclaves, he urged launching out into
the slums to reach those who most needed the message of God's

love. His followers provided an example of this active sanctification by their work among the poor and needy of North America and the world.

Just as Christ's ministry was to the sick and suffering in body and soul, so also, "God's true followers will be found not only telling the world of a distant heaven but bringing it near to the suffering humanity and lifting up the sorrowing, the poor, the distressed, with the same heart of compassion and the same hand of love."[8]

A Christian's Responsibility

Christianity brings with it responsibility. This is true of the nation as well as the individual. Simpson believed that the Protestant nations—Great Britain, the United States and Germany—had a responsibility to use their superior economies and production capabilities as a blessing to lesser developed countries of the world. With the emergence of the Anglo-Saxon people as the major influence in the world, their duty to spread the gospel was great. He wrote, "This is the race that God has made in a special sense the custodians of His truth and the representative of Christian ideas and principles. This is a very solemn responsibility, and constitutes a very glorious possibility in the religious outlook of our age."[9] The picture of suffering and depravity in heathen lands is painted over and over by Simpson in countless articles about the need for missionary concern. In one such article he wrote, "But yonder, in the dark and dreadful power of heathenism, men are sinking to destruction, women are given over to shame and slavery worse than death, and little children are abandoned to cruelty and wrong without remedy, and we 'forbear' and sit down amid the immunities and comforts we owe to the Gospel of Jesus Christ and say, 'Behold, I knew it not.' "[10]

In a sermon delivered in 1895, he contrasted the needs of people living under the darkness of heathenism with the plenty and privilege of people living under Christianity. He spoke of babies being flung to the dogs, harsh poverty, slavery and the lowly place of women in some societies. He then exhorted his audience,

> Picture all this, put it all together and compare it with your Christian privileges, with your happy homes, with your sweet maidenhood, with your innocent childhood, with the women's rights and immunities, with the deathbed of your child, the sweet and glorious departing of your friends in heaven's hope that await you forever, and oh! ask what right have these to perish? Is it any wonder that the heart of God suffered for them? Is it any wonder that He gave His only begotten Son that they might not perish? What will we give? What will we do? How much do we care?[11]

The woes of human society were seen by Simpson as the responsibility of Christian men and women. In "Look on the Fields," a sermon preached by Simpson at Carnegie Hall in 1899, he said, "We cannot evade the responsibility. We are our brother's keeper." He then listed some of the problems plaguing mankind; opium, intemperance, immorality, the degradation of women, the blight of childhood, slavery and the slave trade, self-torture, cannibalism, heathen wars, neglect and abuse of the sick, castes, illiteracy, dishonest and false religions.[12] He presented Christianity as the only remedy for all of these human problems. He argued that Christianity should be given to these people before the bad features of Western culture went ahead of the gospel and added to the dark conditions in these societies.[13]

What will it take to save this lost world? Simpson dismissed "mere sentiment" or good intentions and said, "The tenderest love and the most self-denying sacrifices cannot lift our lost humanity from the fearful effects of the fall." What was needed was a divine compassion and a "gospel of superhuman power." This would elevate humanity to a higher level of living. "Human nature is helpless and the very essence of the Gospel is that it gives the power to choose and do right. It has the power to cleanse, purify and uplift human nature."[14] Simpson firmly believed in the power of Christ to regenerate individuals, and, in so doing, to regenerate nations.

The Worth of the Individual

There were those who were saying that the heathen were not worth saving. Simpson gave their "brutal" argument: "These swarming myriads of stupid, ignorant and brutal heathen are just the offscouring, the scum, the vermin of society, and are better left to their inevitable fate to be swept away by the stronger tides of human life on the principle of the 'survival of the fittest.' Like the Indians of our own continent let them die out as inferior races, they are not worth our pains to save."[15] He found this line of thought to be ironic since it came from people whose ancestors had been barbarians until the arrival of the gospel of Christ lifted them out of heathenism.

Those who were writing off the heathen as not worth saving were among those who, adapting Darwin's "survival of the fittest," were saying that the individual was entirely responsible for his status in life. The poor were mired in poverty because they were lazy and lacked the initiative to better themselves. Magnuson called attention to the important contribution of gospel welfare workers on this point.

An important result of the recognition of the social
causes of poverty is a changed attitude toward the
destitute. If the causes of poverty are social rather than
personal, the grounds for blaming the poor are
removed. Moreover, because prejudiced attitudes con-
tribute significantly to injustice, their reshaping is
probably as important to social reform as is the reshaping of unjust social and economic structures. And at this
essential point of attitude, gospel rescue workers were
the most notable, not only in accepting the dispossessed
with compassion and optimism, but in energetically
proclaiming their worth to all who would hear. . . .
Partly as a result of the extensive first-hand experience
that made gospel welfare workers understand clearly the
social causes of poverty and crime, and partly because
concern for others was at the heart of their religious
experience and teaching, rescue groups accepted the
destitute as worthy and capable persons.[16]

Simpson shared the view that the causes of social ills were
often far beyond the control of individuals. He saw the individuals he ministered to, in American slums and in im-
poverished nations overseas, as victims rather than culprits. He
knew that as social and moral conditions became worse, more
and more people would be affected. The assessment of the
attitudes of gospel welfare workers toward the needy, given by
Magnuson, applies to Simpson and his followers. "All of them
deserve acceptance and a second chance . . . given that, the
overwhelming majority would become happy useful citizens.
Nor should the poor be blamed or punished for their poverty.
Assistance ought to be gracious and prompt, providing much-
needed help without offense or pauperization."[17]

Simpson gave his views on true Christian service in a sermon delivered at Old Orchard, Maine in 1908. He said,

> True Christian service means these things. First, entire consecration to God, involving our utter surrender and His ownership of us. God is asking men today not to give Him their service, but themselves. . . . Second, stewardship, that is, disposing of your means He has entrusted to you for His cause and glory and at His direction. . . . Everything is held for God in true consecration and used at His direction and for His glory. Third, the baptism of the Holy Ghost with power for service, and such special gifts as the great Head of the Church and Executive of the Godhead sees to be best fitted for special work assigned to each of His servants with the one supreme gift of love as the essential one for every worker. And fourth, edification and evangelization. That includes the ministry of help in all its forms and the work of soul-winning everywhere.[18]

Love As the Motivation for Service

Behind the social action of Simpson and his followers was the love instilled within them by their living relationship with God through Jesus Christ. Love was the supreme motivation for each Christian's service for God. Love toward fellow humans flowed from the indwelling Christ. Love was to govern every aspect of life. As Simpson wrote, "The great principle of social righteousness and practical consecration is the law of love."[19]

The world needed to see the love of God manifested in the lives and ministries of Christian people. This would stand in stark contrast to the selfishness of the age. "The World's Needs," a sermon preached in 1900, explained, "How we can thus love people." Simpson listed three reasons to love the unlovely people of the world. 1) "We love them because they are dear to Him; because He cares for them." 2) "You can love them because they can be so noble and good. When they become Christians they become such glorious Christians." 3) "We can love them with the love of pity. We can love them because they need the compassion of Jesus Christ."[20]

The love of the Christian is to be an unselfish love, a love that goes out to others freely. Simpson wrote, "The supreme law of the universal love and the essence of love is to think of others and especially of the most needy and helpless ones."[21]

Magnuson, in *Salvation in the Slums*, discusses Simpson and others like him who ministered in the urban centers of America in the late-nineteenth and early-twentieth centuries:

> Entering the slums, then, to help the poor spiritually, these evangelists found conditions that drove them to extend their help across a much wider range of needs. Staying to help, that very extension of aid progressively enlarged their knowledge, resulting in continuing improvements in both the range and effectiveness of their assistance. But the question rises—why did they stay to help? They might well have left in disgust or discouragement, or staying, might have been content only to exhort or rebuke. The answer in considerable measure seems to be that they helped because of a general large-heartedness tied closely to the central emphasis they placed on the Wesleyan doctrine of "holiness" or perfect love.[22]

Love was a motivating force for the outreach of Simpson. Magnuson notes, "Evangelists in the slums displayed a marked ability and willingness to express affection. A.B. Simpson repeatedly referred to his co-workers and others as 'dear brother' or 'beloved brothers.' His Negro associates were his 'beloved colored brethren.' "[23] Simpson saw love as the outgrowth of a life given over to Christ. Love was to be extended to all because God's message of salvation was open to all.

Commenting on the motivation of gospel welfare workers in reaching the needy, Magnuson writes, "Self-sacrifice was another characteristic that conditioned and helped clarify the slum evangelist's idea of the nature of Christian love." He continues, "A.B. Simpson of the Alliance declared sacrifice 'the highest quality of love,' the willingness to make any sacrifice, even for the most unlovely person was at the heart of the divine love which they must have."[24]

"Am I my brother's keeper?" was the text of Simpson's sermon "Mutual Responsibility," which he delivered at Asbury Park in the summer of 1894. Mutual responsibility was described as an essential of human society. Men live in mutual dependence in order to survive. Simpson stated, ". . . if your neighbor is left in ignorance you cannot escape the contact and contagion in some form or measure. We are, therefore, bound to each other by obligations and relations as real and strong as the constitution of nature and the character of God." He explained what it meant to be our brother's keeper. "It means most obviously that we should keep from doing our brother harm, either in his material, physical, social or spiritual interests." Conversely, "It means that we should do good to our brother as we have opportunity. It is not enough to avoid injuring another, but God is constantly giving us opportunities of helping and benefiting one another." Our special obligation beyond this, he noted, is to "seek to save the soul of our brother."[25]

Simpson laid down the principle of love as the motivation for relating to our brother. Who did Simpson say our brother was? Our brother, he pointed out, is not only family members but neighbors, anyone we come into contact with and unseen neighbors in other lands.[26] Simpson called attention to the need of Christians to be concerned about all humans and to avoid cloistering themselves into tight, little religious communities. He urged them to know about the needs of their "brothers" wherever they may live. That was the purpose of his magazines, to make the needs of the world known. He charged Christians in America with the tremendous responsibility of sharing Christianity with the entire world. They were not to keep all of its benefits for themselves. That is why he called attention to wars, floods, famines and social problems. He was attempting to shake a selfish church into thinking about the needs of others. He wrote, "We need to know the needs of our perishing brethren and the fearful conditions of the heathen world. You have no business to plead ignorance if a neighbor were starving next door. You ought to know."[27]

Personal Salvation Versus Social Salvation

While the new theology of his day was urging men to live by a higher law by imitating Christ, Simpson was urging people to have a personal relationship with Christ. Personal salvation and an internal change of heart would then alter the way people related to one another. "The Christian life is not an imitation of Christ," he noted, "but a direct new creation in Christ and the union with Christ is so complete that He imparts His own nature to us and lives His own life in us and then it is not imitation, but simply the outgrowth of the nature implanted within. We live like Christ because we have the Christ-life."[28]

This radical new way of living is consistent with the biblical gospel message and Christianity's traditional conservative theology. Individual salvation logically precedes the transformation of society, according to this paradigm. This was the pattern of history as Christianity spread and changed the world. It changed nation after nation as individual people entered into new life in Christ. Simpson called it ". . . a religion that remedies the wrongs of society by making not society good, but individual men good, which takes them up one by one and then reforms society by reforming the individual."[29] The rescue mission work, the work in hospitals and prisons, the preaching to the poor, the orphanages, the missionary activities and every aspect of the outreach ministries started or influenced by Simpson, all had as their goal the personal conversion of individuals to Christ. Needs were met with the expectation that Christ could be shared with each person ministered to. Food was given in the name of the Lord, not only so that the hungry were fed but so that they might see Christ and his love in the act and be drawn to Christ for salvation from sin. This was the real force for change in society according to Simpson.

As individuals were converted and the Holy Spirit gained full control of their lives, they were not to sit back and take it easy. Simpson argued that, "Spiritual results such as these must lead to practical usefulness."[30] That was the reason why the Alliance and other groups touched by Simpson's message did not sit back but actively engaged in all types of social activities, with spiritual results expected. They had been repeatedly charged to go out and minister to the needy because they themselves had their needs met by Christ.

Confronting American Christians with Social Needs

Simpson sought to confront the churches of America with the needs of the world. In his magazines he called attention to the starving, the poor, the abused, the orphaned and the needy. He spoke of the injustices of foreign societies and of American society as well. "The Practical Hope of the Lord's Coming," a sermon he preached in 1910, brought together his ideas on social conditions and the soon return of Christ. He said of the poor, "Go to the sweat shops of our manufacturing cities, see the poor, attenuated women and children that are toiling for a pittance in suffocating workrooms with long hours of half-remunerated toil." To the rich he said, "You can hoard your money if you please, you can enjoy the banquet and the song if you will, you can grind the face of the poor and compel them to toil on your hard terms . . . but remember that God is bringing you to judgment . . . all the witnesses will meet you face to face some day, and then how you will wish that you could live your life once again." The poor will find relief at Christ's coming, the Christian worker will find reward, but, Simpson warned, the wicked oppressor will find judgment and punishment.[31]

An Evaluation of Simpson's Social Attitude

David O. Moberg, writing about social responsibility and the Christian, has pointed out that the Christian should not, and, indeed cannot, remain neutral on the social issues of his day. One of two positions is indicated by neutrality, according to Moberg, either "that their spiritual message is totally irrelevant to practical problems," or their policy of inaction "conveys, implicitly an endorsement of the status quo." He added, "Approval of the status quo usually is the equivalent of approving the vested interests of power and wealth, implying that such persons are always morally right in social controversies."[32]

Simpson cannot be accused of neutrality on the social issues of his day. He felt that his message applied to the world in which he ministered. He spoke out on a wide range of social issues, both in the United States and in the world at large. While social

reform and the expectation that human society could be perfected was not the thrust of his message social relief was present
to a significant extent. Even though it was always in the context
of personal evangelism, social concern was a part of the theology
and ministry of Simpson and his early followers.

Moberg has given several reasons why evangelical Protestants
have "played down the social implications of the gospel."[33] It
would do well to see how Simpson stands up to Moberg's
criticism.

Moberg has noted that evangelical Protestants "have reacted
against the errors of those theologically liberal religious leaders
who identified the Christian message with a call for social
reform."[34] Without a doubt Simpson was against those who set
out to equate Christianity with social reform. He made that
quite clear on a number of occasions, most notably in *The Old
Faith and the New Gospels* (1911). On the other hand, he did
not abandon programs that involved social relief simply because
theologically liberal clergymen advocated social reform in the
place of personal salvation. The multitude of social service
efforts in which Simpson was involved testify to that. He did,
however, warn that Christian effort detached from advocating
personal regeneration was not really Christian. Mere social
reform was not the remedy for social problems if personal
salvation was ignored.

"Evangelicals have sometimes misinterpreted the prophecy
that perilous times shall come in the last days," Moberg notes.
"They have pessimistically taken this to mean that no matter
what Christians and other men do, conditions will go from bad
to worse; therefore it is no use trying to do anything about social
problems except to rescue souls through personal evangelism."[35]
Simpson shared the viewpoint that world conditions were
bound to get worse. As he wrote on the eve of World War I,

"The Lord said things would be worse and worse as the end drew near. . . . You are not going to see a perfect church. You are not going to see an ideal world. . . . His return is the only remedy for earth's wrongs, the only Paradise this lost world can ever know."[36] He was, however, spared from inaction by his belief that Christ's return was contingent in part upon human efforts to evangelize the world. Only when the gospel had been preached in all the world would Christ return. While this view sided with those who held a "rescue boat" view of Christianity, it did not share all of their pessimism and inaction. For, in the process of evangelization, Simpson and his followers engaged in social welfare work as part of soul-winning, and as an outgrowth of their compassion for human need.

Simpson shared the belief held by his associate, Henry Wilson, that hard times tended to direct individuals to God for help. Wilson, writing in the economically perilous year 1894, observed, "Now storms do drive people to 'cover.' Whether they be atmospheric or financial, spiritual or temporal, one blessing of them is that some at least seek after God in the storm who seldom think of Him in the sunshine."[37] Since personal salvation was the main emphasis of Simpson's message, anything that drove people to God was, necessarily, good. Earthquakes, famines and wars, destructive and harmful as they were, were cited by Simpson as beneficial toward the evangelization of individuals. While Simpson and his movement sought to alleviate human suffering where they encountered it, there was always this element of seeing conditions as beneficial if people were thereby made aware of the need for personal salvation. The giving of social aid, while springing from hearts of genuine compassion, was never totally disassociated from an intense concern for evangelism.

Moberg notes that, "It is assumed that the 'social' and

'personal' aspects of the Christian message, as well as its 'this worldly' and 'other worldly' implications, are opposed as black is to white, and that conversion is solely 'personal' and relevant to the future life."[38] Although Simpson was enthralled with "other worldly" notions, this did not totally blind him to the problems of "this world." He believed that the underlying basis of all human suffering was the fact of evil corrupting this world. Unless the spiritual root of evil was dealt with adequately, he saw no end to social inequities. He wrote, "This is an unequal age. Right is often on the scaffold, and wrong seems ever on the throne. The facts of human life are pathetic, are tragic, are heartbreaking. I find out things enough every year of my life to make memory a storehouse of horror, the cruelties and wrongs that go unrighted . . . the victims that suffer from the oppressor, and there is none to help." His ultimate solution to the problem of evil and suffering was the return of Christ, when "He will break in pieces the oppressor" and aid will come to the help-less.[39] Simpson did not believe in the redemption of human society apart from the physical, premillennial return of Jesus Christ to establish his kingdom. In the meantime, he did not turn a deaf ear to the cries of those in need; this would have been contrary to his understanding of Christ's mission for the church. He did, however, despair of any universal remedy for human suffering. He advocated ministering to social need where one found oneself, just as Jesus had alleviated suffering and sickness when he encountered it. There could, however, be no grand plan of a utopian society brought about on this earth by human effort. Simpson remained a supporter of "other worldly" solutions, personal salvation for individuals now and societal transformation at Christ's return. At the same time he engaged in social welfare service to alleviate human suffering as it was encountered during the course of world evangelization.

Moberg has charged, "Social implications of the gospel have been avoided because of the assumption that anything which is 'social' is thereby not 'spiritual.' . . . That which pertains to 'worldly' society is wrongly assumed to be outside the direct concern of the gospel."[40] Simpson urged his followers to minister the gospel in every area of their lives. In *The Land of Promise*, he wrote, "the most commonplace occupation, the most secular calling, the most trifling act of earthly duty may involve the highest ministry for Christ."[41] Later, in the same book, he wrote, "The highest Christian life should ever be found in contact with the lowest sinfulness and the deepest need."[42] Every role in life could be used to change the world for Christ as believers lived out their lives of love and service.

The gospel applied to the secular and social aspects of life, according to Simpson, even though he concerned himself mostly with spiritual matters. He saw the need for the Christian faith to produce changes in society, to right wrongs. He believed that, "Christianity revolutionizes man's relation to his fellowman." He noted, "Already the spirit of Christianity infused into human society to a certain degree has swept away the curse of slavery, the degradation of women, the blight of childhood, and innumerable social evils which had oppressed the world."[43] Christianity would change society but this change was always linked by Simpson to changing men and women through personal salvation and sanctification. Personal salvation would never reach proportions that would radically alter the makeup of human society. While total transformation of this world awaited Christ's return, human suffering, alcoholism, prostitution, famine, etc. could be confronted and gains could be made in correcting some of the evils of human society.

Moberg has stated, "the 'gospel of individual piety' has interfered with Christian social concern. . . . All too often, waiting for His coming has taken the place of working until His coming. . . . Evangelical churches have looked inward, seeing their own needs almost exclusively. They have stressed the fellowship of believers rather than the ministry of service. . . . Reacting against the liberal doctrines which include the universal fatherhood of God and brotherhood of man, evangelicals have tended to forget that all men are brothers in the flesh even if not in the spirit."[44]

The social aspects of the ministry of A.B. Simpson show a marked concern for those outside of the circle of believers. The hope was that men and women would become Christians through the social concern and love shown by Simpson and his fellow-workers. But even those who did not come to embrace Christianity were given aid. The early Alliance movement was an outgoing, outreach ministry in the slums of America's cities and on foreign mission fields. Repeatedly Simpson called for workers to forsake the luxury of material security and ornate church buildings and to go in ministry to the forgotten peoples of the world. He saw the end times as being characterized by a movement of the gospel down into the lowest classes of human society. He felt that God was, to a degree, abandoning affluent churches because they were abandoning outreach ministries to the lost and needy world outside of their church walls. He saw God moving by His Spirit among the downtrodden, neglected masses of humanity through the work of churches and parachurch organizations willing to do the demanding work of outreach and evangelization.

On a number of occasions Simpson addressed himself to the absolute worth of the individual. In *Words of Comfort for Tired Ones*, he wrote, ". . . in every human being there is something of infinite value, something that God appreciates, something that brought Christ all the way from heaven to die, and that something we can find in every soul and make it a point of contact to better things."[45] While adhering to the doctrine of man's depravity, he saw in mankind a raw material for godliness. He did not limit his concern to safe Christian circles, although the deeper Christian life and sanctification was one of his main concerns. Rather, he called on his followers to launch out into larger society to evangelize the world.

Moberg feared that ". . . there is a deep-seated feeling among evangelicals that 'politics is dirty.' Since social action in democratic societies involves political activity, and political activity requires compromise and thus failure to achieve that which is ideal, it has been felt that the church's purity would be threatened by social action."[46]

The Christian's Civil Responsibilities

Speaking of the Christian's civil responsibilities Simpson wrote, "The New Testament always recognizes the existing conditions of human society, and among them, the fact and right of civil government."[47] He thereby sided with the traditional Christian viewpoint supporting secular government as a divinely ordained control on the political and social areas of human existence. He also wrote, "No true Christian can be an anarchist. While there is an extreme of spread-eagle patriotism, there is also a middle ground of Christian loyalty which recognizes the powers that be as ordained of God, and even when they are not altogether as they should be, submits and supports 'for the Lord's.' " Support for government was unquestioned for him even when one did not agree with everything that one's government was doing. Christians should not evade politics, especially in the United States and other democracies where they have a voice in government. He said, ". . . the individual Christian [is] responsible for his part in good government, for if the people be the kings and their elective voice determines the quality of government, surely no sincere Christian can be indifferent or neglect concerning his civic duties."[48]

While urging Christians to work for good government and not to avoid politics, Simpson warned that things might not always work out for the best. He saw the danger of compromise, which Moberg noted. In an editorial dealing with municipal elections in New York City in 1895, Simpson bemoans the set-back for the forces of good government in their fight against corrupt politicians. He felt, however, that an important lesson had been learned "that good men need never expect to gain anything by compromise. The friends of good government can only hope to succeed when they take their stand on principles of uncompromising righteousness and refuse to touch hands with political intriguers, and pander to popular license for the sake of votes."[49] He would be among those who contributed to the view propounded by later evangelicals that politics is "dirty." However, where he saw good being done in government he pointed it out in his publications. In 1908 he wrote, "It is an interesting and stirring sight to behold an honest public man like our State Governor Charles E. Hughes, by sheer force of moral worth and intellectual weight winning his way in this day of weak, time-serving men in spite of the political bosses . . ."[50]

While politics was a dirty matter, the individual, Simpson believed, must continue to take an interest in and applaud the good being done by government. He told a group of women who were working and praying for the conversion of large numbers of policemen in New York City, that ". . . God would interpose in some wonderful way to bring to light the awful abuses of the whole system, and cleanse the administration of our whole police department."[51]

While Simpson falls among those Moberg accuses of fostering

an attitude of politics being "dirty" and the compromising of Christian principles being wrong, Simpson did not want to see the cause of political reform abandoned by Christians. They should, he urged, speak out in support of the forces of good and condemn that which they saw as wrong, rather than evading civic responsibility entirely. Evangelical believers should work for better government while, at the same time, not expect to help usher in a man-made utopia.

Of greater concern to Simpson was the dissolution of respect for authority and the toppling of the monarchies of Europe. He was fearful of democracy. In 1918, the year before his death, he wrote, "The last form of government is democracy; it is anarchy; it is license; it is liberty gone mad, and in the frightful tragedy Satan leaps into the saddle and drives the horses to the last tribulation. That is what he is going to do. That is what he is trying to do in every revolution." He believed that revolutions were going to usher in the Antichrist spoken of in the book of Revelation.[52] Writing in 1901 he noted, "There have never been such disturbances politically as in these latter times. . . . Within twenty years there have been assassinated or assailed a score of royal personages and rulers of Europe and America, and our country supposed to be the refuge for the oppressed, and home of the free, has surpassed all other nations in its record of monstrous atrocity." He concluded, "We may execute the criminal and hunt down the anarchist, but the thing is there, seething, foaming and ready to burst in some form under the surface."[53] He saw the rise of democracy, the overthrow of monarchies by revolutions and, in his view, the total collapse of obedience to authority as signs of the end times. He expected the immediate return of Christ. This picture of world society at the turn of the century painted by Simpson was dark. It totally contradicted the optimistic picture of human progress being heralded by liberal religious leaders. But Simpson felt that his views were consistent with the prophetic accounts he found in the Bible.

Simpson had little use for socialism. In 1909 he wrote, "The essential idea of socialism at its best is that the individual is submerged in the community and the whole is more important than any single part." This idea, he said, came close to the idea of Christians as members of the body of Christ, all being of equal value. This, however, was the only point of agreement he could find between Christianity and socialism, which he labeled a "false system."[54]

While politics was for Simpson an essentially "dirty" activity Christians were urged to obey civil government and work against evil and for good. The rise of democracies frightened him because he saw anarchism as a danger and felt that world society was being readied for the Antichrist. One senses a tone of remorse in Simpson's writings toward the end of his life as monarchies were being destroyed in Europe. With the fall of monarchies he saw authority in the person of a single authority figure within each state slipping away under the surging tides of popular revolutions. Clearly he was much more comfortable with monarchies than with democracy. These Tory views may stem from his early life in Canada under the crown. It may also, however, be due to his fondness for the notion of kingship derived from his support of the divine kingship of God over the universe. Indeed, one finds little talk of political democracy in the Bible. He saw the rise of democracy, populism and socialism, therefore, as signs that the world system was falling apart and that God would soon intervene in human history.

The Combining of the Spiritual and the Social

With the world system falling apart and social needs on the

rise, evangelicals were not united in what to do. The result was social inaction on the part of evangelicals, a position that Moberg is critical of. He points out "... other forms of 'separate from the world' also helped to account for social neglect. A modern form of monasticism has led some to try to live completely apart from worldly people. . . . To avoid contamination from sin, social life has been divorced from the spiritual life. Salvation has been presented as applying only to the 'soul' of man."[55]

A.B. Simpson's position was certainly not the evangelical norm for his day. While He believed and taught personal holiness and separation from evil and The Christian and Missionary Alliance was part of the Holiness Movement in America in the late nineteenth century, Simpson did not teach that Christians should be isolated from the world, rather they should launch out into the world with the Christian message of hope and redemption. This was the thrust of his missionary outreach as well as his domestic efforts. His followers lived and worked in slums, "red-light districts," along dock fronts and among poor immigrant groups. He urged his workers to go to the lower class masses both at home and abroad. Unlike some holiness preachers in his day, he believed that God called Christians to be in the world but not of the world. He preached personal holiness but not social isolation, for if the Christian was to evangelize the world he must go where the people were, in the world. Yet, Simpson emphasized, the world system must not be internalized by the believer. The true Christian always endorsed a higher system than the world and saw the need for rejecting the evil influences that sought to drag the faithful down into the quicksand of "worldliness."

The life of the Christian outlined by Simpson was one of involvement in the world while having an inward holiness that enabled one to remain detached from all that was evil in the world and, therefore, to be able to assist others to accept Christ and live holy lives. Reacting to the extreme separation being urged by some he wrote, "There is always the danger of going to extremes. Some people are so spiritual that they would take God out of the secular realm and leave it wholly to the devil and the world. Now, just because Satan claims to be god of this world God wants us to recognize Him in it and inscribe 'Holiness to the Lord' upon everything we touch."[56]

He said of holiness, "Not a holiness so cold and inaccessible that poor sinners will feel that it is too high for their attainment, and too hard for their helplessness to reach: but a gospel holding out to all classes and conditions of sinful men the constant proclamation of a Saviour."[57] His desire was that "every consecrated heart, every circle of professed holiness might be a city of refuge, where poor sinners would know that they would ever find a welcome. This is the service to which Christ is calling His consecrated people."[58] Christians were made holy not so that they could gather together to enjoy their holiness, but to launch out in Christian service to the world.

Moberg perceived that the lack of involvement by evangelicals in social concerns might be a result of the rising economic standards among evangelicals which caused them to become content with the status quo.[59] This point applies more specifically to the period after Simpson's death and contributed, it is felt by some, to the dearth of evangelical social work from the 1920s onward. Simpson, however, continually attacked the wealthy churches of his day. He saw them as abandoning the lower classes. He believed that all Christians should reach out to others across class lines. His views are a stinging indictment of much of later evangelicalism. Even though his followers were not all from the lower classes, in fact they were largely middle class, they all saw their mission to be to the neglected masses of the world. Significant social work was done by those who had previously lived in isolation from the slums and poorer quarters of the cities.

Simpson would be in essential agreement with Moberg's point that "It is a sin not to be concerned about the needs of suffering mankind, and it is selfish to say that Christians must keep 'pure' in God's sight by avoiding 'worldly problems.' " As well as his statement that, "Lack of Christ-like compassion is a symptom of spiritual death."[60]

Simpson had often charged the church of his day with ignoring the poor while they lived in luxury and worshiped in splendid church buildings. He attacked those who had become so spiritually dead and in tune with the world that human suffering and need failed to touch them. He repeatedly characterized the Alliance as a movement "downward to the masses," and as a movement intended to awaken the larger Church to the needs that were being ignored. Yet he did espouse some doctrines that could be taken to extremes by those who followed him; that personal salvation was the main concern of evangelism, that holiness meant a degree of separation from the world, that politics was a "dirty" area and compromise a step toward spiritual ruin, and that Christ's return was soon to correct all social ills.

Should Simpson be faulted for fostering ideas which would later be taken to extremes he did not intend and used to buttress the neglect of social problems by later evangelicals? In *The Great Reversal*, Moberg charges, "The intense interest in social service on the part of early Christian and Missionary Alliance members was soon subtly opposed by its founder, possibly because this competed with institutional goals of the new fellowship."[61] He gives no specific examples for the "subtle" opposition of Simpson to social work.

There is in the material written toward the end of Simpson's life less of an emphasis on social concerns and, indeed, by the end of his life some of the social welfare work was being curtailed. Orphanages were phased out as children grew to adulthood and left the facilities and some Alliance works were taken over by others.

Conclusion

Social concern was never at the center of the message or the ministry of A.B. Simpson. Nor was social work at the center of the work of The Christian and Missionary Alliance. Simpson was primarily an evangelist, a missionary organizer, a pastor and a publisher. He was interested in seeing souls saved from sin by the power of Christ. He emphasized the conservative theological doctrine of personal salvation. As a result Simpson could never be called a social reformer. That was not how he saw himself; that was not what the record shows.

What social activity Simpson and his followers became involved in was on a personal level. It was a person-to-person, compassionate concern for needy individuals. Simpson had no overall social plan to reform society. He saw social needs and attempted to aid its victims on an individual basis. It was never his intention to try to make this world over into a utopian society. He differed sharply, as we have seen, from those who had this as their goal.

Coming into New York City, which was teeming with poor people and being flooded with immigrants, Simpson responded to human needs. When sending missionaries to foreign countries and encountering social ills, he sought to alleviate human suffering. When social wrongs were encountered in foreign societies he spoke out against them. The saving of souls meant coming into contact with hunger, poverty and social displacement. Simpson did not ignore these problems. He fed people, he gave the poor job training, he rescued alcoholics, he reclaimed fallen women, he clothed, fed and housed orphans and sent food to famine stricken countries. But righting social ills was only a side-effect of evangelization. It resulted from the love of God being lived out in the life of Simpson and his followers. Love sent him and his co-workers into neglected areas and caused them to respond to human need with hearts full of compassion.

Society was not going to radically change for the better. Consistent with his premillennialism, Simpson believed that the world would become increasingly worse until it would be replaced by the kingdom of God to be ushered in by Christ's triumphant, physical return to earth. The most pressing physical needs encountered by Simpson and his followers were met. Larger social structure and economic problems were beyond his direct involvement, although he did not remain entirely silent about them.

Social work was done by Simpson and those he influenced. This has been documented. Social change was not the goal of his ministry; spiritual change was. Simpson called on fellow evangelicals to stay in the world to win it for Christ. He preached sanctification, but not social isolation. It would be wrong to think of him as a fundamentalist, advocating the extreme social isolation that the term implies. Individual purity and consecration were to enable each believer to become a more effective Christian worker. Purity and consecration did not mean monasticism but, rather, service.

It would be fair to conclude that the social activity of Simpson and his followers, while flowing from deep compassion, love and personal concern was always seen by them as a stop-gap effort to meet human needs until Christ returned to right all wrongs. Their work, however, was praiseworthy, whatever the intention of their ultimate evangelistic designs were. Simpson and other evangelicals who did social work in the late nineteenth and early twentieth centuries stand in stark contrast to the rigidly separated and isolated fundamentalists and the many later evangelicals who benignly neglected social problems.

Endnotes

1. A.B. Simpson, "The Right and Wrong Way of Living," *The Christian and Missionary Alliance*, 22 July 1905: 453.
2. A.B. Simpson, "In Trust With the Gospel: In Debt to the World," *The Christian and Missionary Alliance*, 8 Jan. 1897: 31.
3. A.B. Simpson, "The Highest Service," *Christian Alliance*, 2 Feb. 1894: 114.
4. A.B. Simpson, "The Commission and the Anointing," *Christian Alliance*, 27 July, 1894: 77.
5. A.B. Simpson, "God's Compensation," *The Christian and Missionary Alliance*, 25 June 1897: 605-606.
6. A.B. Simpson, "Consecration in Relation to Our Duty to the Weak and Erring," *Christian Alliance*, 6 July 1894: 4.
7. A.B. Simpson, "The Cities of Refuge or The Sinner's Inheritance," *Christian Alliance*, 5 Jan. 1895: 4.
8. A.B. Simpson, "The Gospel Work," *The Christian and Missionary Alliance*, 24 Sept. 1904: 258.
9. A.B. Simpson, "Providence and Missions," *The Christian and Missionary Alliance*, 20 July 1898: 53.
10. A.B. Simpson, "Emergency, Opportunity, Responsibility," *The Christian and Missionary Alliance*, 7 Sept. 1901: 130.
11. A.B. Simpson, "God So Loved," *Christian Alliance*, 23

Oct. 1895: 265.

12. A.B. Simpson, "Look on the Fields," *The Christian and Missionary Alliance*, 15 Oct. 1899: 344-346.

13. Simpson, *Missionary Messages*, (New York: Christian Alliance Publishing Co., 1925) 14.

14. Simpson, *Messages* 54, 56.

15. Simpson, *Messages* 88-89.

16. Norris Magnuson, *Salvation in the Slums*, (Metuchen, NJ: Scarecrow Press, 1977) 176.

17. Magnuson 177.

18. A.B. Simpson, "Present Truth," *The Christian and Missionary Alliance*, 15 Aug. 1908: 332.

19. A.B. Simpson, "Consecration in Relation to Our Social Duties," *Christian Alliance*, 29 June 1894: 699.

20. A.B. Simpson, "The World's Needs," *The Christian and Missionary Alliance*, 22 Sept. 1906: 181.

21. A.B. Simpson, "Helped to Help Others," *The Christian and Missionary Alliance*, 16 Sept. 1899: 258.

22. Magnuson 38.

23. Magnuson 39.

24. Magnuson 41.

25. A.B. Simpson, "Mutual Responsibility," *Christian Alliance*, 17 Aug. 1894: 148-149.

26. Simpson, "Mutual" 150.

27. Simpson, *Messages* 91.

28. A.B. Simpson, "The Highest Christian Life," *Christian Alliance*, 3 Aug. 1894: 101.

29. Simpson, *Messages* 110.

30. A.B. Simpson, "The World for Christ: A New Departure," *The Christian and Missionary Alliance*, 23 Apr. 1897: 388.

31. A.B. Simpson, "The Practical Hope of the Lord's Coming," *The Christian and Missionary Alliance*, 6 Aug. 1910:

305-306.

32. David O. Moberg, *Inasmuch: Christian Social Responsibility in the Twentieth Century* (Grand Rapids: Eerdman's, 1965) 14.

33. Moberg 18.

34. Moberg 19.

35. Moberg 19.

36. A.B. Simpson, "Living Under the Power of the World," *The Alliance Weekly*, 21 Feb. 1914: 324.

37. Henry Wilson, "The Wings of God for 1894," *Christian Alliance*, 5 Jan. 1894: 7.

38. Moberg 19.

39. Simpson, "Living" 324.

40. Moberg 20.

41. A.B. Simpson, *The Land of Promise* (New York: Christian Alliance Publishing Co., n.d.) 178.

42. Simpson, *Promise* 185.

43. Simpson, "Turning the World Upside Down," *The Alliance Weekly*, 26 July 1913, 259.

44. Moberg 20.

45. A.B. Simpson, *Words of Comfort for Tired Ones* (New York: Alliance Press Co., 1903) 61-62.

46. Moberg 20.

47. A.B. Simpson, "Christian Consecration in Relation to Our Civil and Social Duties," *Christian Alliance*, 29 June 1894: 697.

48. Simpson, *Comfort* 64.

49. A.B. Simpson, "Practical Lessons from Political Overturnings," *Christian Alliance*, 13 Nov. 1895: 312.

50. A.B. Simpson, editorial, *The Christian and Missionary Alliance*, 7 Aug. 1895: 88.

51. A.B. Simpson, "Answered Prayer," *Christian Alliance*, 7

Aug. 1895: 88.

52. A.B. Simpson, "Overlapping of the Coming Age," *The Alliance Weekly*, 19 Jan. 1918: 243.

53. A.B. Simpson, "The Outlook of the Age," *The Christian and Missionary Alliance*, 12 Oct. 1901: 201.

54. A.B. Simpson, "Christian Altruism," *The Christian and Missionary Alliance*, 7 Aug. 1909: 315.

55. Moberg 20-21.

56. A.B. Simpson, "Prayer for Temporal Needs," *The Christian and Missionary Alliance*, 19 Nov. 1898: 469.

57. Simpson, *Promise* 193.

58. Simpson, *Promise* 194.

59. Moberg 21.

60. Moberg 22.

61. David O. Moberg, *The Great Reversal* (New York: Lippincott, 1972) 31.

EPILOGUE

North American evangelicals should be justifiably proud of the social relief activities of our immediate predecessors in the faith. We should not allow the theologically liberal Protestant establishment to deprive us of our history by claiming the evangelical tradition of social consciousness in the nineteenth century as entirely their own. Certainly the roots of both traditions have been profoundly impacted by late nineteenth century Protestant responses to social dislocation. It is my hope that this book has brought to light the strong sense of purpose and the active social agenda on the part of the evangelical tradition influenced by A.B. Simpson and The Christian and Missionary Alliance.

However, if all we learn from the past are interesting facts which increase our pride and give us a sense of history, we are only going half the way toward reclaiming our evangelical heritage. Looking back with pride and greater understanding should challenge today's believers to respond to the social problems faced by Christ's Church as we near the turn of the century.

Since the reawakening of the social consciousness of evangelicals there has been a renewal of commitment to accept responsibility for the physical needs of those less fortunate in this world. For the most part this renewed interest has not lost sight of the primary duty of the Church which is to bring the saving gospel of Jesus Christ to fallen humanity.

The society founded by Simpson, The Christian and Missionary Alliance, never really stopped being socially concerned, at least in its overseas missionary operations. It has consistently committed itself to medical missionary activity. Even when other mission boards doubted the validity of medical work, the Alliance kept nurses and doctors in the field staffing clinics and hospitals.

More recently the denomination has reorganized its relief activities under the umbrella of CAMA Services Inc. The central work of this arm of the worldwide ministry of The Christian and Missionary Alliance is refugee assistance. It maintains relief work in Southeast Asia, West Africa and the Middle East, feeding the hungry, clothing the naked, providing medical assistance to the ailing and housing the homeless. All of these ministries have been within the larger agenda of sharing Christianity's message of eternal hope with those in temporal discomfort.

Local Alliance churches in North America have often responded to those in need in their communities as well. Relief for flood and hurricane victims, soup kitchens and other social outreach programs have shown that meeting the physical needs of people usually gives believers an opening to share their personal faith in Christ with those to whom a helping hand is being lent. What an opportunity is around us today with poverty on the rise, the social problems caused by the increase in broken homes, and crime, AIDS and various other social needs seemingly at an overwhelming level in our society. What a time for the Church to reach out in love offering care and hope and the saving gospel of Jesus Christ.

Unfortunately, the residue of fundamentalist isolationism still lingers on the fringes of evangelicalism at the end of the twentieth century. There are still those who have qualms about engaging the church in social relief efforts. To those who remain unconvinced of the importance of the church to be about the business of ministering to the "whole man" I would say, look to our immediate evangelical heritage and look at the words of our Lord. I challenge anyone to find a lessened commitment to evangelism on the part of Simpson and the early Christian and Missionary Alliance because they were involved in social relief operations. Quite to the contrary, their large-hearted response to the spiritual and physical needs of the people of their day can serve as a model for us.

In many ways we face social dislocations as disruptive and personally devastating as believers of one hundred years ago. May we respond as they did, by showing the love of the Lord for suffering humanity. "Whatever you did for one of the least of these brothers of mine, you did for me" (Matthew 25:40). May we too hear our Lord's command "Well done, good and faithful servant!" (25:21).

Bibliography

Books Written by A.B. Simpson

The Coming One. New York: Christian Alliance Publishing Co., 1912.

The Four-Fold Gospel. New York: Christian Alliance Publishing Co., 1925.

The Gospel of the Kingdom. New York: Christian Alliance Publishing Co., 1890.

Is Life Worth Living? South Nyack, NY: Christian Alliance Publishing Co., 1899.

The Land of Promise. New York: Christian Alliance Publishing Co., 1888.

Missionary Messages. New York: Christian Alliance Publishing Co., 1925.

The Old Faith and the New Gospels. New York: Christian Alliance Publishing Co., 1911.

Words of Comfort for Tired Ones. New York: Alliance Press Co., 1903.

Articles Written by A.B. Simpson

"Annual Report of the President and General Superintendent of the Christian and Missionary Alliance." *The Christian and Missionary Alliance,* 6 June 1908: 155.

"Answered Prayer." *Christian Alliance,* 7 Aug. 1895: 88.

"Aggressive Christianity." *Christian Alliance,* 27 Nov. 1895: 345-346.

"Aggressive Christianity." *The Christian and Missionary Alliance,* 15 Sept. 1900: 148-149.

"Christ and Caste." *The Word, Work and World,* Mar. 1882: 122.

"Christ's Coming the Key to All Questions of the Age." *The Christian and Missionary Alliance,* 9 Mar. 1898: 228-229.

"Christian Altruism." *The Christian and Missionary Alliance,* 7 Aug. 1909: 315.

"Christian Consecration in Relation to Our Civil and Social Duties." *Christian Alliance,* 29 June 1894: 697.

"A Church Within a Church." *Christian Alliance,* 29 May 1895: 344.

"Consecration in Relation to the Weak and Erring." *Christian Alliance*, 6 July 1894: 5.

"Consecration in Relation to Our Social Duties." *Christian Alliance*, 29 June 1894: 699.

"Cuban Relief." *The Christian and Missionary Alliance*, 30 Mar. 1898: 301.

"Distinctive Teachings." *The Word, Work and World*, July 1887: 3.

"Editorial." *The Christian and Missionary Alliance*, 15 Jan. 1897: 60.

"Editorial." *The Christian and Missionary Alliance*, 12 Mar. 1897: 252.

"Editorial." *The Christian and Missionary Alliance*, 7 May 1897: 444.

"Editorial." *The Christian and Missionary Alliance*, 29 Aug. 1908: 362.

"Emergency, Opportunity, Responsibility." *The Christian and Missionary Alliance*, 7 Sept. 1901: 130-131.

"God So Loved." *Christian Alliance*, 23 Oct. 1895: 265.

"God's Compensation." *The Christian and Missionary Alliance*, 25 June, 1897: 606.

"How the Church Can Reach the Masses." *The Word, Work and World*, Jan. 1882: 24-25.

"In Trust With the Gospel; In Debt to the World." *The Christian and Missionary Alliance*, 8 Jan. 1897: 31.

"Is War Right?" *The Christian and Missionary Alliance*, 4 May 1898: 421.

"Living Under the Power of the World." *The Alliance Weekly*, 21 Feb. 1914: 324.

"Look Unto the Fields." *The Christian and Missionary Alliance*, 28 Oct. 1899: 344-346.

"Missions and Premillennialism." *The Christian and Missionary Alliance*, 26 Oct. 1898: 396-397.

"Mutual Responsibility." *Christian Alliance*, 17 Aug. 1894: 148-149.

"Our Trust." *The Christian and Missionary Alliance*, 28 May 1910: 146-147.

"Overlapping of the Coming Age." *The Alliance Weekly*, 19 Jan. 1918: 243.

"Practical Lessons from Political Overturnings." *Christian Alliance*, 13 Nov. 1895: 312.

"Prayer for Temporal Needs." *The Christian and Missionary Alliance*, 19 Nov. 1898: 469.

"President's Report of the Work of the Christian and Missionary Alliance." *The Christian and Missionary Alliance*, 5 June 1909: 154.

"Providence and Missions." *The Christian and Missionary Alliance*, 20 July 1898: 53-54.

"Separation." *Christian Alliance*, 11 Sept. 1895: 170.

"Signs of the Times." *The Christian and Missionary Alliance*, 23 Feb. 1898: 180-181.

"The Armenian Outrages." *Christian Alliance*, 14 Dec. 1894: 55.

"The Christian Age." *The Alliance Weekly*, 10 Feb. 1912: 291.

"The Cities of Refuge." *Christian Alliance*, 5 Jan. 1894: 4.

"The Coming King." *Christian Alliance*, 27 Apr. 1894: 455.

"The Commission and the Anointing." *Christian Alliance*, 27 July 1894: 76-77.

"The Conservation of the Forces and Resources of Our Work." *The Alliance Weekly*, 13 Apr. 1912: 19.

"The Curse of Selfishness." *The Christian and Missionary Alliance*, 17 Sept. 1904: 254.

"The Dark Side and Bright Side of Christmas." *Christian Alliance*, 25 Dec. 1895: 412.

"The Gospel in Cuba and the Philippines." *The Christian and Missionary Alliance*, 20 July 1898: 76.

"The Gospel of Work." *The Christian and Missionary Alliance*, 24 Sept. 1904: 258.

"The Hand of God in Our National Conflict." *The Christian and Missionary Alliance*, 18 May 1898: 468.

"The Highest Christian Life." *Christian Alliance*, 3 Aug. 1894: 101.

"The Highest Service." *Christian Alliance*, 2 Feb. 1894: 114.

"The Lord's Coming and Missions." *The Christian and Missionary Alliance*, 31 Aug. 1907: 98.

"The Ministering Church." *The Christian Alliance and Missionary Weekly*, 13 Mar. 1893: 163-165.

"The Mission of the Alliance." *The Christian and Missionary Alliance*, 4 Nov. 1899: 365.

"The Outlook of the Ages." *The Christian and Missionary Alliance*, 12 Oct. 1901: 201.

"The Outlook in the East." *Christian Alliance*, 18 Dec. 1895: 387.

"The Parables of the Kingdom." *The Christian and Missionary Alliance*, 26 Dec. 1903: 45.

"The Perils of the Modern Church." *The Christian and Missionary*

Alliance, 8 Jan. 1897: 34-35.

"The Practical Hope of the Lord's Coming." *The Christian and Missionary Alliance*, 6 Aug. 1910: 305-306.

"The Pre-millennial Coming of the Lord." *Christian Alliance*, 10 Aug. 1894: 130.

"The Progress of the War." *The Christian and Missionary Alliance*, 4 May 1898: 420.

"The Progress of the War." *The Christian and Missionary Alliance*, 11 May 1898: 444.

"The Progress of the War." *The Christian and Missionary Alliance*, 15 June 1898: 564.

"The Prospect of Peace." *The Christian and Missionary Alliance*, 3 Aug. 1898: 108.

"The Quest of Wisdom." *The Christian and Missionary Alliance*, 5 June 1909: 164.

"The Religious Wants of New York." *The Word, Work and World*, Jan. 1882: 26-28.

"The Rich and the Poor Meet Together." *The Word, Work and World*, Jan. 1882: 25.

"The Right and the Wrong Way of Living." *The Christian and Missionary Alliance*, 22 July 1905: 453.

"The Second Coming of Christ." *The Word, Work and World*, Nov. 1885: 315-316.

"The Significance of Our Times." *Christian Alliance*, 19 Oct. 1894: 373-374.

"The Significance of the Spanish-American War." *The Christian and Missionary Alliance*, 27 Apr. 1898: 396.

"The Situation in the West Indies." *The Christian and Missionary Alliance*, 6 Apr. 1898: 314-315.

"The Turkish Question." *Christian Alliance*, 13 Nov. 1895: 444.

"The War Cloud Overhanging Europe." *The Christian and Missionary Alliance*, 12 Nov. 1898: 444.

"The World for Christ: A New Departure." *The Christian and Missionary Alliance*, 23 Apr. 1897: 388-389.

"The World's Needs." *The Christian and Missionary Alliance*, 22 Sept. 1906: 181.

"War Clouds." *The Christian and Missionary Alliance*, 2 Mar. 1898: 204.

"Who Is Our Brother?" *Christian Alliance*, 17 Aug. 1894: 150.

Unsigned Articles

"Berachah Orphanage." *The Christian and Missionary Alliance*, Apr. 1899: 145.

"Famine in Central Russia." *Christian Alliance*, 5 Nov. 1895: 426.

"Field Notes." *Christian Alliance*, 25 Dec. 1895: 412.

"Field Notes." *The Christian and Missionary Alliance*, May 1899: 190.

"Field Notes." *The Christian and Missionary Alliance*, 3 June 1899: 62.

"Field Notes." *The Christian and Missionary Alliance*, 19 Aug. 1899: 190.

"Jerry McAuley's Crenmore Mission." *The Word, Work and World*, June 1883: 92.

"Opium in Western China." *The Christian and Missionary Alliance*, 26 Oct. 1898: 402.

"Opening of the Hephzibah House." *Christian Alliance*, 19 Jan. 1894: 77.

"Our Work in Denver." *The Christian and Missionary Alliance*, 8 June 1898: 544-545.

"Plague in Alexandria." *The Christian and Missionary Alliance*, 2 Dec. 1899: 435.

"Reports of Christian Work." *The Word, Work and World*, Oct. 1886: 239-245.

"Reports of the Home Work." *Christian Alliance*, 17 Aug. 1894: 161.

"Rescue Mission Day at the New York Convention." *Christian Alliance*, 16 Oct. 1895: 253.

"The Bowery Mission." *The Word, Work and World*, Jan. 1887: 34.

"The City Mission of Williamsport, Pa." *The Christian and Missionary Alliance*, 26 Mar. 1897: 304.

"The Kingdom Come." *The Alliance Weekly*, 24 Oct. 1914: 51.

"Turning the World Upsidedown." *The Alliance Weekly*, 26 July 1913: 259.

"Women's Branch of the City Mission." *The Word, Work and World*, Mar. 1887: 145.

"Work Among the Fallen." *The Word, Work and World*, Feb. 1882: 75.

"Wrongs of Indian Womanhood." *The Christian and Missionary Alliance*, 10 Nov. 1900: 257.

Other Articles

Agnew, Miss M. "Rescue Mission Work." *The Christian and Missionary Alliance*, 1 June 1901: 305.

Brickensteen, Miss E.M. "A Special Call to the Children of the

Junior Alliance." *The Christian and Missionary Alliance*, 19 Feb. 1897: 182.

Farr, F.W. "Antidotes for Anti-Semitism." *The Christian and Missionary Alliance*, Jan. 1898: 40.

Funk, A.E. "The Homes and Institutions of the Alliance." *The Christian and Missionary Alliance*, 23 Apr. 1897: 393-394.

Gibbord, Charles. "The Florence Mission." *The Word, Work and World*, Nov. 1885: 308.

Hadley, S.H. "Rescue Missions at the Convention." *Christian Alliance*, 25 Sept. 1896: 286.

Naylor, Mrs. Henry. "First National Convention of Christian Workers." *The Word, Work and World*, July 1886: 32.

"First National Convention of Christian Workers." *The Word, Work and World*, Aug. 1886: 95-98.

"Midnight Mission on Twenty-seventh Street." *The Word, Work and World*, June 1883: 91.

Pannell, C.H.H. "Annual Report of the Secretary of the Christian Alliance." *Christian Alliance*, 6 Nov. 1895: 300.

Parmenter, Mary F. "The Condition of Women in China." *The Christian and Missionary Alliance*, 23 Dec. 1899: 470-471.

Rainsford, W.S. "Preaching the Gospel to the Poor." *The Word, Work and World*, Nov. 1885: 312-314.

Schultz, Mr. O.S. "Berachah Orphanage." *Christian Alliance*, 23 Nov. 1894: 495-496.

"Berachah Orphanage." *Christian Alliance*, 29 May 1895: 348.

Simpson, J.G.H. "Old Water Street." *The Christian and Missionary Alliance*, 5 Dec. 1903: 12.

Steele, Mrs. A.S. "Steele Home for Needy Children." *Christian Alliance*, 9 Oct. 1895: 236.

Wilson, Henry. "The Magdalen Home." *The Christian and Missionary Alliance*, 19 Jan. 1898: 64.

"The Wings of God for 1894." *Christian Alliance*, 5 Jan. 1894: 7.

Biographical Source Books

Dahms, John V. "The Social Interest and Concern of A.B. Simpson." *The Birth of a Vision.* eds., David F. Hartzfeld and Charles Nienkirchen. Beverlodge, Alberta: Buena Book Services, 1986.

Niklaus, Robert K., John S. Sawin and Samuel J. Stoesz. *All for Jesus: God at Work in the Christian and Missionary Alliance Over One Hundred Years.* Camp Hill, PA: Christian Publications, 1986.

Pardington, George P. *Twenty-five Wonderful Years 1889-1914.* New York: Christian Alliance Publishing Co., 1914.

Stoesz, Samuel J. *Understanding My Church*. Harrisburg: Christian Publications, Inc., 1968.

Thompson, A.E. *A.B. Simpson: His Life and Work*. Harrisburg: Christian Publications, Inc., 1920 (revised edition, 1960).

Tozer, A.W. *Wingspread: A.B. Simpson: A Study in Spiritual Altitude*. Harrisburg: Christian Publications, Inc., 1943.

Religious Background Source Books

Brewster, Chauncey B. *The Kingdom of God and American Life*. New York: Thomas Whittaker, Inc., 1912.

Cutting, R. Fulton. *The Church and Society*. New York: Macmillan, 1912.

Dayton, Donald. "Preface." *Salvation in the Slums*, Norris Magnuson. Metuchen, NJ: Scarecrow Press, 1977.

Dombrowski, James. *The Early Days of Christian Socialism in America*. New York: Columbia Univ. Press, 1936.

Gladden, Washington. *How Much Is Left of the Old Doctrines?* Boston: Houghton, Mifflin, 1899.

Handy, Robert T. *A Christian America*. New York: Oxford Univ. Press, 1971.

Henry, Carl F.H. *The Uneasy Conscience of Modern Fundamentalism* Grand Rapids: Eerdmans, 1947.

Herron, George D. *The New Redemption.* New York: Thomas Y. Crowell, 1893.

Hodges, George. *Faith and Social Service.* New York: Thomas Whittaker Inc., 1896.

Hollinger, Dennis P. *Individualism and Social Ethics: An Evangelical Syncretism.* Lanham, MD: University Press of America, 1983.

Hopkins, Charles H. *The Rise of the Social Gospel in American Protestantism 1865-1915.* New Haven: Yale Univ. Press, 1940.

Marsden, George M. *Fundamentalism and American Culture: The Shaping of Twentieth-Century Evangelicalism: 1870-1925.* New York: Oxford U. Press, 1980.

Magnuson, Norris. *Salvation in the Slums.* Metuchen, NJ: The Scarecrow Press, 1977.

Matthews, Douglas K. "Approximating the Millennium: Toward a Coherent Premillennial Theology of Social Transformation." diss., Waco, TX: Baylor University, 1992.

May, Henry F. *Protestant Churches and Industrial America.* New York: Harper, 1949.

Moberg, David O. *Inasmuch: Christian Social Responsibilty in the Twentieth Century.* Grand Rapids: Eerdman's, 1965.

——. *The Great Reversal.* New York: Lippincott, 1972.

Rauschenbusch, Walter. *Christianity and the Social Crisis*. New York: Macmillan, 1907.

———. *Christianizing the Social Order*. New York: Macmillan, 1912.

———. *Dare We Be Christians?* Boston: Pilgrim Press, 1914.

———. *Unto Me*. Boston: Pilgrim Press, 1912.

Sandeen, Ernest R. *The Roots of Fundamentalism*. Chicago: Univ. of Chicago Press, 1970.

Smith, Timothy L. *Revivalism and Social Reform*. New York: Abingdon, 1957.

Strong, Josiah. *The Next Great Awakening*. New York: Baker & Taylor, 1902.

———. *The Twentieth Century City*. New York: Baker & Taylor, 1898.

Synan, Vinson. *The Holiness-Pentecostal Movement in the United States*. Grand Rapids: Eerdman's, 1971.

Weber, Timothy P. *Living in the Shadow of the Second Coming: American Premillennialism 1875-1925*. New York: Oxford U. Press, 1979.

White, Ronald C. Jr. and C. Howard Hopkins. *The Social Gospel*. Philadelphia: Temple Univ. Press, 1976.

Woodbridge, John D., Mark A. Noll and Nathan O. Hatch. *The Gospel in America: Themes in the Story of America's Evangelicals* Grand Rapids: Zondervan, 1979.